ISBN: 9781314372168

Published by:
HardPress Publishing
8345 NW 66TH ST #2561
MIAMI FL 33166-2626

Email: info@hardpress.net
Web: http://www.hardpress.net

Riverside College Classics

THE SECOND BOOK OF MODERN VERSE

A SELECTION FROM THE WORK
OF CONTEMPORANEOUS AMERICAN POETS

EDITED BY

JESSIE B. RITTENHOUSE

*Editor of The Little Book of American Poets
and The Little Book of Modern Verse*

HOUGHTON MIFFLIN COMPANY

BOSTON   NEW YORK   CHICAGO   SAN FRANCISCO
The Riverside Press Cambridge

The Riverside Press
CAMBRIDGE . MASSACHUSETTS
PRINTED IN THE U . S . A

FOREWORD

IT was my intention, when preparing *The Little Book of Modern Verse*, published in 1913, to continue the series by a volume once in five years, but as it seemed inadvisable to issue one during the war, it is now six years since the publication of the first volume.

In the meantime, that the series might cover the period of American poetry from the beginning, *The Little Book of American Poets* was edited, confined chiefly to work of the nineteenth century, but ending with a group of living poets whose work has fallen equally within our own period. This group, including Edwin Markham, Bliss Carman, Edith Thomas, Louise Imogen Guiney, Lizette Woodworth Reese, and many others whose work has enriched both periods, was fully represented also in *The Little Book of Modern Verse;* and it has seemed necessary, therefore, keenly as I regret the necessity, which limits of space impose, to omit the work of all poets who have been represented in both of my former collections.

Indeed the period covered by the present volume has been so prolific that it became necessary, if one would represent it with even approximate adequacy, to forego including many poets from *The Little Book of Modern Verse* itself, and but twenty-eight are repeated from that collection.

Even with these necessary eliminations in the interest of space for newer poets, the general scheme of the series — that of small, intimate volumes that shall be typical of the period, rather than exhaustive — has made it impossible to include all whose work I should otherwise have been glad to represent.

3109

While I have not hesitated, where a poet's earlier work seemed finer and more characteristic than his later, to draw upon such earlier work, in the main *The Second Book of Modern Verse* has been selected from poetry published since 1913, the date of my first anthology.

JESSIE B. RITTENHOUSE

NEW YORK
September 23, 1919

CONTENTS

Abraham Lincoln walks at Midnight. *Vachel Lindsay* . 157
Acceptance. *Willard Wattles* 26
Ad Matrem Amantissimam et Carissimam Filii in Æter-
    num Fidelitas. *John Myers O'Hara* 203
After Apple-Picking. *Robert Frost* 185
After Sunset. *Grace Hazard Conkling* 86
Afternoon on a Hill. *Edna St. Vincent Millay* . . 84
Afterwards. *Mahlon Leonard Fisher* 203
Ambition. *Aline Kilmer* 127
Ancient Beautiful Things, The. *Fannie Stearns Davis* . 128
Apology. *Amy Lowell* 178
April on the Battlefields. *Leonora Speyer* . . . 168
April — North Carolina. *Harriet Monroe* 14
Atropos. *John Myers O'Hara* 213
Autumn. *Jean Starr Untermeyer* 186
Autumn Movement. *Carl Sandburg* 188

Ballad of a Child. *John G. Neihardt* 124
Behind the House is the Millet Plot. *Muna Lee* . . 182
Berkshires in April. *Clement Wood* 6
Beyond Rathkelly. *Francis Carlin* 78
Birches. *Robert Frost* 91
Bitter Herb, The. *Jeanne Robert Foster* 181
Blind. *Harry Kemp* 13
Blue Squills. *Sara Teasdale* 8
Breaking, The. *Margaret Steele Anderson* 29

Chanson of the Bells of Osenèy. *Cale Young Rice* . . 25
Chant of the Colorado, The. *Cale Young Rice* . . 96
Child in Me, The. *May Riley Smith* 141
Chinese Nightingale, The. *Vachel Lindsay* . . . 37
Choice. *Angela Morgan* 75
Cinquains. *Adelaide Crapsey* 206

City, The. *Charles Hanson Towne* 94
City Roofs. *Charles Hanson Towne* 55
Compensation. *William Ellery Leonard* 65
Convention. *Agnes Lee* 111
Cradle Song. *Josephine Preston Peabody* 121

Dark Cavalier, The. *Margaret Widdemer* 199
Day before April, The. *Mary Carolyn Davies* . . . 6
Days. *Karle Wilson Baker* 82
Death — Divination. *Charles Wharton Stork* . . . 201
Dialogue. *Walter Conrad Arensberg* 180
Dilemma. *Orrick Johns* 31
Doors. *Hermann Hagedorn* 193
Dream. *Anna Hempstead Branch* 20
Dream of Aengus Og, The. *Eleanor Rogers Cox* . . 73
Dusk at Sea. *Thomas S. Jones, Jr.* 51

Earth. *John Hall Wheelock* 9
Earth's Easter. *Robert Haven Schauffler* 169
Ellis Park. *Helen Hoyt* 82
Enchanted Sheepfold, The. *Josephine Preston Peabody* 67
Envoi. *Josephine Preston Peabody* 119
Evening Song of Senlin. *Conrad Aiken* 99
Exile from God. *John Hall Wheelock* 208
Eye-Witness. *Ridgely Torrence* 56

Falconer of God, The. *William Rose Benét* . . . 30
"Feuerzauber." *Louis Untermeyer* 90
Fields, The. *Witter Bynner* 170
Fifty Years Spent. *Maxwell Struthers Burt* . . . 93
First Food, The. *George Sterling* 134
Flammonde. *Edwin Arlington Robinson* 33
Flower of Mending, The. *Vachel Lindsay* 71
Four Sonnets. *Thomas S. Jones, Jr.* 22
Francis Ledwidge. *Grace Hazard Conkling* . . . 167

Gift, The. *Louis V. Ledoux* 128
Girl's Songs, A. *Mary Carolyn Davies* 66

CONTENTS

General William Booth Enters into Heaven. *Vachel Lindsay* 63

God's Acre. *Witter Bynner* 62

God's World. *Edna St. Vincent Millay* 188

Good-Bye. *Norreys Jephson O'Conor* 77

Good Company. *Karle Wilson Baker* 90

Great Hunt, The. *Carl Sandburg* 179

Harbury. *Louise Driscoll* 52

Have you an Eye. *Edwin Ford Piper* 184

Heat. *H. D.* 102

Hill Wife, The. *Robert Frost* 116

Hills of Home. *Witter Bynner* 209

Homeland, The. *Dana Burnet* 120

How much of Godhood. *Louis Untermeyer* . . . 134

Hrolf's Thrall, His Song. *Willard Wattles* . . . 144

"I am in Love with High Far-Seeing Places." *Arthur Davison Ficke* 74

I have a Rendezvous with Death. *Alan Seeger* . . 164

"I Pass a Lighted Window." *Clement Wood* . . . 192

Idealists. *Alfred Kreymborg* 12

Idol-Maker prays, The. *Arthur Guiterman* . . . 28

"If you should tire of loving me." *Margaret Widdemer* . 70

Indian Summer. *William Ellery Leonard* . . . 199

In Excelsis. *Thomas S. Jones, Jr.* 7

In the Hospital. *Arthur Guiterman* 27

In the Monastery. *Norreys Jephson O'Conor* . . . 191

In the Mushroom Meadows. *Thomas Walsh* . . . 80

In Patris Mei Memoriam. *John Myers O'Hara* . . 202

In Spite of War. *Angela Morgan* 170

Interlude. *Scudder Middleton* 69

Interpreter, The. *Orrick Johns* 145

Invocation. *Clara Shanafelt* 20

Irish Love Song. *Margaret Widdemer* 194

Jerico. *Willard Wattles* 173

Kings are passing Deathward, The. *David Morton* . . 173

Lady, A. *Amy Lowell* 140
Last Piper, The. *Edward J. O'Brien* 209
Lincoln. *John Gould Fletcher* 153
Little Things. *Orrick Johns* 18
Loam. *Carl Sandburg* 208
Lonely Burial. *Stephen Vincent Benét* , . . 164
Lonely Death, The. *Adelaide Crapsey* . . . 207
Love is a Terrible Thing. *Grace Fallow Norton* . . 47
Love Song, A. *Theodosia Garrison* 119
Love Songs. *Sara Teasdale* 45
Lover envies an Old Man, The. *Shaemas O Sheel* . . 69
Lynmouth Widow, A. *Amelia Josephine Burr* . . 54

Madonna of the Evening Flowers. *Amy Lowell* . . 103
Mad Blake. *William Rose Benét* 111
Mater Dolorosa. *Louis V. Ledoux* 132
Men of Harlan. *William Aspinwall Bradley* . . 182
Monk in the Kitchen, The. *Anna Hempstead Branch* . 135
Morning Song of Senlin. *Conrad Aiken* . . . 87
Most-Sacred Mountain, The. *Eunice Tietjens* . . 95
Moth-Terror. *Benjamin De Casseres* 212
Mould, The. *Gladys Cromwell* 202
Music I heard. *Conrad Aiken* 50
Muy Vieja Mexicana. *Alice Corbin* 143

Name, The. *Anna Hempstead Branch* 112
Narrow Doors, The. *Fannie Stearns Davis* . . 191
New Dreams for Old. *Cale Young Rice* . . . 19
New God, The. *James Oppenheim* 104
Nirvana. *John Hall Wheelock* 195
Note from the Pipes, A. *Leonora Speyer* . . . 83
Nun, A. *Odell Shepard* 196

Of One Self-Slain. *Charles Hanson Towne* . . . 110
Old Age. *Cale Young Rice* 212
Old Amaze. *Mahlon Leonard Fisher* 85

Old King Cole. *Edwin Arlington Robinson* 145
Old Manuscript. *Alfred Kreymborg* 98
Old Ships. *David Morton* 51
Omnium Exeunt in Mysterium. *George Sterling* . . 211
Open Windows. *Sara Teasdale* 84
Orchard. *H. D.* 101
Our Little House. *Thomas Walsh* 120
Overnight, a Rose. *Caroline Giltinan* 27
Overtones. *William Alexander Percy* 189

Path Flower. *Olive Tilford Dargan* 15
Path that leads to Nowhere, The. *Corinne Roosevelt*
   Robinson 81
Patterns. *Amy Lowell* 105
Peace. *Agnes Lee* 172
Pierrette in Memory. *William Griffith* 204
Poets. *Joyce Kilmer* 26
Prayer during Battle. *Hermann Hagedorn* . . . 158
Prayer of a Soldier in France. *Joyce Kilmer* . . 159
Prevision. *Aline Kilmer* 132
Provinces, The. *Francis Carlin* 210

Reveillé. *Louis Untermeyer* 29
Richard Cory. *Edwin Arlington Robinson* . . . 109
Road not taken, The. *Robert Frost* 3
Romance. *Scudder Middleton* 76
Rouge Bouquet. *Joyce Kilmer* 165
Runner in the Skies, The. *James Oppenheim* . . . 99

Saint's Hours, A. *Sarah N. Cleghorn* 139
Silence. *Edgar Lee Masters* 196
Silent Folk, The. *Charles Wharton Stork* . . . 110
Slumber Song. *Louis V. Ledoux* 124
Smith, of the Third Oregon, dies. *Mary Carolyn Davies* . 162
Son, The. *Ridgely Torrence* 142
Song. *Margaret Steele Anderson* 76
Song. *Adelaide Crapsey* 205
Song. *Edward J. O'Brien* 163

Song. *Margaret Widdemer* 181
Song of two Wanderers, A. *Marguerite Wilkinson* . 79
Songs of an Empty House. *Marguerite Wilkinson* . . 115
Spoon River Anthology. *Edgar Lee Masters* . . 148
Spring. *John Gould Fletcher* 4
Spring in Carmel. *George Sterling* 48
Spring Song. *William Griffith* 5
Students. *Florence Wilkinson* 175
Symbol. *David Morton* 3

Tampico. *Grace Hazard Conkling* 177
"There will come Soft Rain." *Sara Teasdale* . . . 5
Three Sisters. *Arthur Davison Ficke* 205
Thrush in the Moonlight, A. *Witter Bynner* . . . 100
To a Portrait of Whistler in the Brooklyn Art Museum.
    Eleanor Rogers Cox 32
To Any one. *Witter Bynner* 172
Trees. *Joyce Kilmer* 12

Unknown Belovèd, The. *John Hall Wheelock* . . . 205

Valley Song. *Carl Sandburg* 48
Venus Transiens. *Amy Lowell* 72
Voyage à l'Infini. *Walter Conrad Arensberg* . . . 86

Wanderer, The. *Zoë Akins* 52
Water Ouzel, The. *Harriet Monroe* 97
When the Year grows Old. *Edna St. Vincent Millay* . 189
Where Love is. *Amelia Josephine Burr* 68
Where Love once was. *James Oppenheim* . . . 194
Which. *Corinne Roosevelt Robinson* 177
White Comrade, The. *Robert Haven Schauffler* . . 159
Wide Haven. *Clement Wood* 171
Wind Rose in the Night, A. *Aline Kilmer* . . . 133

Yellow Warblers. *Katharine Lee Bates* 13
You. *Ruth Guthrie Harding* 74

ACKNOWLEDGMENTS

THANKS are due to the following publishers, editors, and individual owners of copyright for their kind permission to include selections from the volumes enumerated below:

To the estate of Edmund Brooks for a selection from "A Lark Went Singing," by Ruth Guthrie Harding.

To the Century Company for selections from "Trails Sunward," "Wraiths and Realities," and "Collected Poems" of Cale Young Rice; "Challenge" by Louis Untermeyer; "Songs for the New Age" and "War and Laughter" by James Oppenheim; and for "After Sunset" by Grace Hazard Conkling, from the *Century Magazine*.

To the Cornhill Company for selections from "The Divine Image," by Caroline Giltinan.

To Messrs. E. P. Dutton & Co. for selections from "The Retinue, and Other Poems," by Katharine Lee Bates (copyright, 1918), "Lanterns in Gethsemane," by Willard Wattles (copyright, 1918), and "The Earth Turns South," by Clement Wood (copyright, 1919).

To Messrs. Dodd, Mead & Co. for selections from "A Masque of Poets," edited by Edward J. O'Brien.

To Messrs. George H. Doran Company for selections from "Joyce Kilmer: Poems, Essays and Letters," edited by Robert Cortes Holliday (copyright, 1918); "Candles That Burn," by Aline Kilmer (copyright, 1919); "The Dreamers," by Theodosia Garrison (copyright, 1917); "Fifes and Drums" (copyright, 1917); "The Roadside Fire" (copyright, 1912) and "In Deep Places" (copyright, 1914). by Amelia Josephine Burr; "To-Day and To-Morrow" (copyright, 1916) and "World of Windows" (copyright, 1919), by Charles Hanson Towne.

To The Four Seas Company for selections from "The Charnel Rose," by Conrad Aiken.

To Messrs. Henry Holt & Co. for selections from "North

of Boston" and "Mountain Interval," by Robert Frost; "Chicago Poems" and "Cornhuskers," by Carl Sandburg; "These Times," by Louis Untermeyer; "Portraits and Protests," by Sarah N. Cleghorn; "The Factories, and Other Poems" and "The Old Road to Paradise," by Margaret Widdemer; and "My Ireland," by Francis Carlin.

To Messrs. Houghton Mifflin Company for selections from "Rose of the Wind," by Anna Hempstead Branch; "The Singing Leaves" and "Harvest Moon," by Josephine Preston Peabody; "A Sister of the Wind," by Grace Fallow Norton; "Sea Garden," by H. D.; for the poem "Lincoln," by John Gould Fletcher, from "Some Imagist Poets, 1917"; "In the High Hills," by Maxwell Struthers Burt; "Old Christmas and Other Kentucky Tales," by William Aspinwall Bradley; "Turns and Movies," by Conrad Aiken; "A Lonely Flute," by Odell Shepherd; "Idols," by Walter Conrad Arensberg; and to the *Atlantic Monthly* for the use of "The Ancient Beautiful Things" and "The Narrow Doors," by Fannie Stearns Davis.

To Messrs. Harper & Bros. for selections from "Poems," by Dana Burnet, "The Mirthful Lyre," by Arthur Guiterman, and for the poem "There Will Come Soft Rain," by Sara Teasdale, from *Harper's Magazine.*

To Mr. B. W. Huebsch for selections from "Growing Pains," by Jean Starr Untermeyer, and "The Vaunt of Man," by William Ellery Leonard.

To Mr. Mitchell Kennerley for selections from "Renascence and Other Poems," by Edna St. Vincent Millay; "Sonnets of a Portrait Painter" and "The Man on the Hill-Top," by Arthur Davison Ficke; and for the poems, "Blind," by Harry Kemp, and "The Wanderer," by Zoë Akins.

To Mr. Alfred A. Knopf for selections from "Asphalt," by Orrick Johns; "Mushrooms," by Alfred Kreymborg; and "Profiles from China," by Eunice Tietjens.

To the John Lane Company for selections from "Forward, March," by Angela Morgan; "Songs of the Celtic Past," by Norreys Jephson O'Conor; "Singing Fires of Erin," by Eleanor Rogers Cox; and "Gardens Overseas," by Thomas Walsh.

To The Macmillan Company for selections from "The Man Against the Sky," by Edwin Arlington Robinson;

"General William Booth Enters into Heaven, and Other Poems," "The Congo, and Other Poems," and "The Chinese Nightingale and Other Poems," by Vachel Lindsay; "Songs and Satires" and "Spoon River Anthology," by Edgar Lee Masters; "Sword Blades and Poppy Seed," "Men, Women and Ghosts," and "Pictures of the Floating World," by Amy Lowell; "Love Songs," by Sara Teasdale; "Poems and Ballads," by Hermann Hagedorn; "The Story of Eleusis," by Louis V. Ledoux; "The New Day," by Scudder Middleton; "The Drums in Our Street," by Mary Carolyn Davies; and "The Quest," by John G. Neihardt.

To The Midland Press for a selection from "Barbed Wire," by Edwin Ford Piper.

To Mr. Thomas B. Mosher for selections from "The Voice in the Silence," by Thomas S. Jones, Jr.

To Messrs. John P. Morton & Co. for selections from "A Flame in the Wind," by Margaret Steele Anderson.

To The Manas Press for selections from "Verse" by Adelaide Crapsey.

To Messrs. G. P. Putnam's Sons for selections from "The Shadow of Ætna," by Louis V. Ledoux.

To Messrs. Small, Maynard & Co. for selections from "White Fountains," by Edward J. O'Brien.

To Mr. A. M. Robertson for the use of the poem, "Omnium Exeunt," by George Sterling.

To Messrs. Charles Scribner's Sons for selections from "Path-Flower," by Olive Tilford Dargan; "The Children of the Night," by Edwin Arlington Robinson; "One Woman to Another" and "Service and Sacrifice," by Corinne Roosevelt Robinson; "Poems," by Alan Seeger; "Dust and Light," by John Hall Wheelock; and for the poems, "Eye-Witness," by Ridgely Torrence, and "In the Hospital," by Arthur Guiterman, from *Scribner's Magazine*.

To Messrs. Smith & Sale for selections from "Threnodies," by John Myers O'Hara.

To Messrs. Frederick A. Stokes Company for selections from "Grenstone Poems," by Witter Bynner.

To Mr. Robert J. Shores for selections from "The Loves and Losses of Pierrot," by William Griffith.

To Mr. James T. White for selections from "City Pastorals," by William Griffith.

To The Wilmarth Company for selections from "The Shadow Eater," by Benjamin De Casseres.

To the Yale University Press for selections from "The Falconer of God" and "The Burglar of the Zodiac," by William Rose Benét; "Young Adventure" by Stephen Vincent Benét, and "Blue Smoke," by Karl Wilson Baker.

To the *Yale Review* for the use of "Open Windows," by Sara Teasdale.

To Miss Harriet Monroe, editor of *Poetry: A Magazine of Verse*, for the use of the following selections: "Indian Summer," by William Ellery Leonard; "Song," "Let It Be Forgotten," by Sara Teasdale; "The Mould," by Gladys Cromwell; "Ellis Park," by Helen Hoyt; "Harbury," by Louise Driscoll; "Muy Vieja Mexicana," by Alice Corbin Henderson; "Hrolf's Thrall," by Willard Wattles; "Invocation," by Clara Shanafelt; "Peace" and "Convention," by Agnes Lee; "The Millet Plot," by Muna Lee; "Students," by Florence Wilkinson; "Tampico," by Grace Hazard Conkling; "To a Portrait of Whistler in the Brooklyn Art Museum," by Eleanor Rogers Cox; and "April — North Carolina" and "The Water Ouzel," by Harriet Monroe.

To William Stanley Braithwaite for the use of "Spring," by John Gould Fletcher, first published in *The Poetry Review of America*.

To Charles Wharton Stork, editor of *Contemporary Verse*, for "April on the Battlefields," by Leonora Speyer; "Songs of an Empty House," by Marguerite Wilkinson; and for permission to use his own poems, "Death — Divination," and "The Silent Folk."

To *Everybody's Magazine* for permission to use "A Song of Two Wanderers," by Marguerite Wilkinson, and "Old Ships," by David Morton.

To the *Nation* for "A Note from the Pipes," by Leonora Speyer.

To Mahlon Leonard Fisher, editor of *The Sonnet*, for the use of his poems, "Afterwards" and "Old Amaze."

To the *Outlook* for "The White Comrade," by Robert Haven Schauffler.

To the *New Republic* for "The Son," by Ridgely Torrence.

To the *Bellman* for "The Kings are passing Deathward," by David Morton.

THE ROAD NOT TAKEN

Two roads diverged in a yellow wood,
And sorry I could not travel both
And be one traveler, long I stood
And looked down one as far as I could
To where it bent in the undergrowth;

Then took the other, as just as fair,
And having perhaps the better claim,
Because it was grassy and wanted wear;
Though as for that the passing there
Had worn them really about the same,

And both that morning equally lay
In leaves no step had trodden black.
Oh, I kept the first for another day!
Yet knowing how way leads on to way,
I doubted if I should ever come back.

I shall be telling this with a sigh
Somewhere ages and ages hence:
Two roads diverged in a wood, and I —
I took the one less traveled by,
And that has made all the difference.

Robert Frost

SYMBOL

My faith is all a doubtful thing,
  Wove on a doubtful loom, —
Until there comes, each showery spring,
  A cherry-tree in bloom;

And Christ who died upon a tree
That death had stricken bare,
Comes beautifully back to me,
In blossoms, everywhere.

David Morton

SPRING

AT the first hour, it was as if one said, "Arise."
At the second hour, it was as if one said, "Go forth."
And the winter constellations that are like patient
  ox-eyes
Sank below the white horizon at the north.

At the third hour, it was as if one said, "I thirst";
At the fourth hour, all the earth was still:
Then the clouds suddenly swung over, stooped, and
  burst;
And the rain flooded valley, plain and hill.

At the fifth hour, darkness took the throne;
At the sixth hour, the earth shook and the wind
  cried;
At the seventh hour, the hidden seed was sown;
At the eighth hour, it gave up the ghost and died.

At the ninth hour, they sealed up the tomb;
And the earth was then silent for the space of three
  hours.
But at the twelfth hour, a single lily from the gloom
Shot forth, and was followed by a whole host of
  flowers.

John Gould Fletcher

"THERE WILL COME SOFT RAIN"

THERE will come soft rain and the smell of the ground,
And swallows circling with their shimmering sound;

And frogs in the pools singing at night,
And wild plum-trees in tremulous white;

Robins will wear their feathery fire
Whistling their whims on a low fence-wire.

And not one will know of the war, not one
Will care at last when it is done.

Not one would mind, neither bird nor tree,
If mankind perished utterly.

And Spring herself when she woke at dawn,
Would scarcely know that we were gone.

Sara Teasdale

SPRING SONG

SOFTLY at dawn a whisper stole
   Down from the Green House on the Hill,
Enchanting many a ghostly bole
   And wood-song with the ancient thrill.

Gossiping on the country-side,
   Spring and the wandering breezes say,
God has thrown Heaven open wide
   And let the thrushes out to-day.

William Griffith

THE DAY BEFORE APRIL

THE day before April
    Alone, alone,
I walked in the woods
    And I sat on a stone.

I sat on a broad stone
    And sang to the birds.
The tune was God's making
    But I made the words.
                    Mary Carolyn Davies

BERKSHIRES IN APRIL

IT is not Spring — not yet —
But at East Schaghticoke I saw an ivory birch
Lifting a filmy red mantle of knotted buds
Above the rain-washed whiteness of her arms.

It is not Spring — not yet —
But at Hoosick Falls I saw a robin strutting,
Thin, still, and fidgety,
Not like the puffed, complacent ball of feathers
That dawdles over the cidery Autumn loam.

It is not Spring — not yet —
But up the stocky Pownal hills
Some springy shrub, a scarlet gash on the grayness,
Climbs, flaming, over the melting snows.

It is not Spring — not yet —
But at Williamstown the willows are young and
        golden,

Their tall tips flinging the sun's rays back at him;
And as the sun drags over the Berkshire crests,
The willows glow, the scarlet bushes burn,
The high hill birches shine like purple plumes,
A royal headdress for the brow of Spring.
It is the doubtful, unquiet end of Winter,
And Spring is pulsing out of the wakening soil.

Clement Wood

IN EXCELSIS

SPRING!
And all our valleys turning into green,
Remembering —
As I remember! So my heart turns glad
For so much youth and joy — this to have had
When in my veins the tide of living fire
Was at its flow;
This to know,
When now the miracle of young desire
Burns on the hills, and Spring's sweet choristers
        again
Chant from each tree and every bush aflame
Love's wondrous name;
This under youth's glad reign,
With all the valleys turning into green —
This to have heard and seen!

And Song!
Once to have known what every wakened bird
Has heard;
Once to have entered into that great harmony
Of love's creation, and to feel
The pulsing waves of wonder steal

Through all my being; once to be
In that same sea
Of wakened joy that stirs in every tree
And every bird; and then to sing —
To sing aloud the endless Song of Spring!

Waiting, I turn to Thee,
Expectant, humble, and on bended knee;
Youth's radiant fire
Only to burn at Thy unknown desire —
For this alone has Song been granted me.
Upon Thy altar burn me at Thy will;
All wonders fill
My cup, and it is Thine;
Life's precious wine
For this alone: for Thee.
Yet never can be paid
The debt long laid
Upon my heart, because my lips did press
In youth's glad Spring the Cup of Loveliness!
                              Thomas S. Jones, Jr.

BLUE SQUILLS

How many million Aprils came
    Before I ever knew
How white a cherry bough could be,
    A bed of squills, how blue.

And many a dancing April
    When life is done with me,
Will lift the blue flame of the flower
    And the white flame of the tree.

Oh, burn me with your beauty, then,
  Oh, hurt me, tree and flower,
Lest in the end death try to take
  Even this glistening hour.

O shaken flowers, O shimmering trees,
  O sunlit white and blue,
Wound me, that I through endless sleep
  May bear the scar of you.

Sara Teasdale

EARTH

GRASSHOPPER, your fairy song
And my poem alike belong
To the dark and silent earth
From which all poetry has birth;
All we say and all we sing
Is but as the murmuring
Of that drowsy heart of hers
When from her deep dream she stirs:
If we sorrow, or rejoice,
You and I are but her voice.

Deftly does the dust express
In mind her hidden loveliness,
And from her cool silence stream
The cricket's cry and Dante's dream;
For the earth that breeds the trees
Breeds cities too, and symphonies.
Equally her beauty flows
Into a savior, or a rose —

Looks down in dream, and from above
Smiles at herself in Jesus' love.
Christ's love and Homer's art
Are but the workings of her heart;
Through Leonardo's hand she seeks
Herself, and through Beethoven speaks
In holy thunderings around
The awful message of the ground.

The serene and humble mold
Does in herself all selves enfold —
Kingdoms, destinies, and creeds,
Great dreams, and dauntless deeds,
Science that metes the firmament,
The high, inflexible intent
Of one for many sacrificed —
Plato's brain, the heart of Christ:
All love, all legend, and all lore
Are in the dust forevermore.

Even as the growing grass
Up from the soil religions pass,
And the field that bears the rye
Bears parables and prophecy.
Out of the earth the poem grows
Like the lily, or the rose;
And all man is, or yet may be,
Is but herself in agony
Toiling up the steep ascent
Toward the complete accomplishment
When all dust shall be, the whole
Universe, one conscious soul.
Yea, the quiet and cool sod
Bears in her breast the dream of God.

If you would know what earth is, scan
The intricate, proud heart of man,
Which is the earth articulate,
And learn how holy and how great,
How limitless and how profound
Is the nature of the ground —
How without terror or demur
We may entrust ourselves to her
When we are wearied out, and lay
Our faces in the common clay.

For she is pity, she is love,
All wisdom she, all thoughts that move
About her everlasting breast
Till she gathers them to rest:
All tenderness of all the ages,
Seraphic secrets of the sages,
Vision and hope of all the seers,
All prayer, all anguish, and all tears
Are but the dust, that from her dream
Awakes, and knows herself supreme —
Are but earth when she reveals
All that her secret heart conceals
Down in the dark and silent loam,
Which is ourselves, asleep, at home.

Yea, and this, my poem, too,
Is part of her as dust and dew,
Wherein herself she doth declare
Through my lips, and say her prayer.

John Hall Wheelock

TREES

I THINK that I shall never see
A poem lovely as a tree.

A tree whose hungry mouth is prest
Against the earth's sweet flowing breast;

A tree that looks at God all day,
And lifts her leafy arms to pray;

A tree that may in summer wear
A nest of robins in her hair;

Upon whose bosom snow has lain;
Who intimately lives with rain.

Poems are made by fools like me,
But only God can make a tree.

Joyce Kilmer

IDEALISTS

BROTHER Tree:
Why do you reach and reach?
Do you dream some day to touch the sky?
Brother Stream:
Why do you run and run?
Do you dream some day to fill the sea?
Brother Bird:
Why do you sing and sing?
Do you dream —
Young Man:
Why do you talk and talk and talk?

Alfred Kreymborg

BLIND

THE Spring blew trumpets of color;
Her Green sang in my brain —
I heard a blind man groping
"Tap — tap" with his cane;

I pitied him in his blindness;
But can I boast, "I see" ?
Perhaps there walks a spirit
Close by, who pities me, —

A spirit who hears me tapping
The five-sensed cane of mind
Amid such unguessed glories —
That I am worse than blind.

Harry Kemp

YELLOW WARBLERS

THE first faint dawn was flushing up the skies
When, dreamland still bewildering mine eyes,
I looked out to the oak that, winter-long,
— a winter wild with war and woe and wrong —
Beyond my casement had been void of song.

And lo! with golden buds the twigs were set,
Live buds that warbled like a rivulet
Beneath a veil of willows. Then I knew
Those tiny voices, clear as drops of dew,
Those flying daffodils that fleck the blue,

Those sparkling visitants from myrtle isles,
Wee pilgrims of the sun, that measure miles

Innumerable over land and sea
With wings of shining inches. Flakes of glee,
They filled that dark old oak with jubilee,

Foretelling in delicious roundelays
Their dainty courtships on the dipping sprays,
How they should fashion nests, mate helping mate,
Of milkweed flax and fern-down delicate
To keep sky-tinted eggs inviolate.

Listening to those blithe notes, I slipped once more
From lyric dawn through dreamland's open door,
And there was God, Eternal Life that sings,
Eternal joy, brooding all mortal things,
A nest of stars, beneath untroubled wings.

Katharine Lee Bates

APRIL — NORTH CAROLINA

WOULD you not be in Tryon
   Now that the spring is here,
When mocking-birds are praising
   The fresh, the blossomy year?

Look — on the leafy carpet
   Woven of winter's browns
Iris and pink azaleas
   Flutter their gaudy gowns.

The dogwood spreads white meshes —
   So white and light and high —
To catch the drifting sunlight
   Out of the cobalt sky.

The pointed beech and maple,
　　The pines, dark-tufted, tall,
Pattern with many colors
　　The mountain's purple wall.

Hark — what a rushing torrent
　　Of crystal song falls sheer!
Would you not be in Tryon
　　Now that the spring is here?

Harriet Monroe

PATH FLOWER

A RED-CAP sang in Bishop's wood,
　　A lark o'er Golder's lane,
As I the April pathway trod
　　Bound west for Willesden.

At foot each tiny blade grew big
　　And taller stood to hear,
And every leaf on every twig
　　Was like a little ear.

As I too paused, and both ways tried
　　To catch the rippling rain, —
So still, a hare kept at my side
　　His tussock of disdain, —

Behind me close I heard a step,
　　A soft pit-pat surprise,
And looking round my eyes fell deep
　　Into sweet other eyes;

The eyes like wells, where sun lies too,
    So clear and trustful brown,
Without a bubble warning you
    That here's a place to drown.

"How many miles?" Her broken shoes
    Had told of more than one.
She answered like a dreaming Muse,
    "I came from Islington."

"So long a tramp?" Two gentle nods,
    Then seemed to lift a wing,
And words fell soft as willow-buds,
    "I came to find the Spring."

A timid voice, yet not afraid
    In ways so sweet to roam,
As it with honey bees had played
    And could no more go home.

Her home! I saw the human lair,
    I heard the huckster's bawl,
I stifled with the thickened air
    Of bickering mart and stall.

Without a tuppence for a ride,
    Her feet had set her free.
Her rags, that decency defied,
    Seemed new with liberty.

But she was frail. Who would might note
    The trail of hungering
That for an hour she had forgot
    In wonder of the Spring.

So shriven by her joy she glowed
   It seemed a sin to chat.
(A tea-shop snuggled off the road;
   Why did I think of that?)

Oh, frail, so frail! I could have wept, —
   But she was passing on,
And I but muddled, "You'll accept
   A penny for a bun?"

Then up her little throat a spray
   Of rose climbed for it must;
A wilding lost till safe it lay
   Hid by her curls of rust;

And I saw modesties at fence
   With pride that bore no name;
So old it was she knew not whence
   It sudden woke and came;

But that which shone of all most clear
   Was startled, sadder thought
That I should give her back the fear
   Of life she had forgot.

And I blushed for the world we'd made,
   Putting God's hand aside,
Till for the want of sun and shade
   His little children died;

And blushed that I who every year
   With Spring went up and down,
Must greet a soul that ached for her
   With "penny for a bun!"

Struck as a thief in holy place
  Whose sin upon him cries,
I watched the flowers leave her face,
  The song go from her eyes.

Then she, sweet heart, she saw my rout,
  And of her charity
A hand of grace put softly out
  And took the coin from me.

A red-cap sang in Bishop's wood,
  A lark o'er Golder's lane;
But I, alone, still glooming stood,
  And April plucked in vain;

Till living words rang in my ears
  And sudden music played:
Out of such sacred thirst as hers
The world shall be remade.

Afar she turned her head and smiled
  As might have smiled the Spring,
And humble as a wondering child
  I watched her vanishing.
                    Olive Tilford Dargan

LITTLE THINGS

THERE's nothing very beautiful and nothing very gay
About the rush of faces in the town by day,
But a light tan cow in a pale green mead,
That is very beautiful, beautiful indeed . .

And the soft March wind and the low March mist
Are better than kisses in a dark street kissed . . .
The fragrance of the forest when it wakes at dawn,
The fragrance of a trim green village lawn,
The hearing of the murmur of the rain at play —
These things are beautiful, beautiful as day!
And I shan't stand waiting for love or scorn
When the feast is laid for a day new-born . . .
Oh, better let the little things I loved when little
Return when the heart finds the great things brittle;
And better is a temple made of bark and thong
Than a tall stone temple that may stand too long.

Orrick Johns

NEW DREAMS FOR OLD

Is there no voice in the world to come crying,
    "New dreams for old!
    New for old!"?
Many have long in my heart been lying,
    Faded, weary, and cold.
All of them, all, would I give for a new one.
    (Is there no seeker
    Of dreams that were?)
Nor would I ask if the new were a true one:
    Only for new dreams!
    New for old!

For I am here, half way of my journey,
    Here with the old!
    All so old!
And the best heart with death is at tourney,
    If naught new it is told.

Will there no voice, then, come — or a vision —
   Come with the beauty
   That ever blows
Out of the lands that are called Elysian?
   I must have new dreams!
   New for old!

Cale Young Rice

INVOCATION

O GLASS-BLOWER of time,
   Hast blown all shapes at thy fire?
Canst thou no lovelier bell,
   No clearer bubble, clear as delight, inflate me —
Worthy to hold such wine
   As was never yet trod from the grape,
Since the stars shed their light, since the moon
   Troubled the night with her beauty?

Clara Shanafelt

DREAM

BUT now the Dream has come again, the world is as
   of old.
Once more I feel about my breast the heartening
   splendors fold.
Now I am back in that good place from which my footsteps came,
And I am hushed of any grief and have laid by my
   shame.

I know not by what road I came — oh wonderful and
   fair!

Only I know I ailed for thee and that thou wert not
    there.
Then suddenly Time's stalwart wall before thee did
    divide,
Its solid bastions dreamed and swayed and there was
    I inside.

It is thy nearness makes thee seem so wonderful and
    far.
In that deep sky thou art obscured as in the noon, a
    star.
But when the darkness of my grief swings up the
    mid-day sky,
My need begets a shining world. Lo, in thy light am I.

All that I used to be is there and all I yet shall be.
My laughter deepens in the air, my quiet in the tree.
My utter tremblings of delight are manna from the sky,
And shining flower-like in the grass my innocencies lie.

And here I run and sleep and laugh and have no name
    at all.
Only if God should speak to me then I would heed
    the call.
And I forget the curious ways, the alien looks of men,
For even as it was of old, so is it now again.

Still every angel looks the same and all the folks are
    there
That are so bounteous and mild and have not any care.
But kindest to me is the one I would most choose
    to be.
She is so beautiful and sheds such loving looks on me.

She is so beautiful — and lays her cheek against my
     own.
Back — in the world — they all will say, "How happy
     you have grown."
Her breath is sweet about my eyes and she has healed
     me now,
Though I be scarred with grief, I keep her kiss upon
     my brow.

All day, sweet land, I fight for thee outside the goodly
     wall,
And 'twixt my breathless wounds I have no sight of
     thee at all!
And sometimes I forget thy looks and what thy ways
     may be!
I have denied thou wert at all — yet still I fight for
     thee.

Anna Hempstead Branch

FOUR SONNETS

I

SANCTUARY

How may one hold these days of wonderment
     And bind them into stillness with a thong,
     Ere as a fleeting dream they pass along
Into the waste of lovely things forspent;
How may one keep what the Great Powers have sent,
     The prayers fulfilled more beautiful and strong
     Than any thought could fashion into song
Of all the rarest harmonies inblent?

There is an Altar where they may be laid
And sealed in Faith within Its sacred care, —
Here they are safe unto the very end;
For these are of the things that never fade,
Brought from the City that is built four-square,
The gifts of Him who is the Perfect Friend.

II

THE LAST SPRING

THE first glad token of the Spring is here
That bears each time one miracle the more,
For in the sunlight is the golden ore,
The joyous promise of a waking year;
And in that promise all clouds disappear
And youth itself comes back as once before,
For only dreams are real in April's store
When buds are bursting and the skies are clear.

Fair Season! at your touch the sleeping land
Quickens to rapture, and a rosy flame
Is the old signal of awakening;
Thus in a mystery I understand
The deepest meaning of your lovely name —
How it will be in that perpetual Spring!

III

THE GARDEN

BEHIND the pinions of the Seraphim,
Whose wings flame out upon the swinging spheres,
There is a Voice that speaks the numbered years
Until that Day when all comes back to Him;

Behind the faces of the Cherubim,
  Whose smiles of love are seen through broken tears,
  There is a Face that every creature fears,
The Face of Love no veil may ever dim.

O Angels of Glad Laughter and of Song,
  Your voices sound so near, the little wall
    Can scarcely hide the trees that bend and nod;
Unbar the gate, for you have waited long
  To show the Garden that was made for all, —
    Where all is safe beneath the Smile of God.

IV

THE PATH OF THE STARS

Down through the spheres that chant the Name of
      One
  Who is the Law of Beauty and of Light
  He came, and as He came the waiting Night
Shook with the gladness of a Day begun;
And as He came, He said: Thy Will Be Done
  On Earth; and all His vibrant Words were white
  And glistering with silver, and their might
Was of the glory of a rising sun.

Unto the Stars sang out His Living Words
  White and with silver, and their rhythmic sound
    Was as a mighty symphony unfurled;
And back from out the Stars like homing birds
  They fell in love upon the sleeping ground
    And were forever in a wakened world.
                              Thomas S. Jones, Jr.

CHANSON OF THE BELLS OF OSENÈY
Thirteenth Century

THE bells of Osenèy
(Hautclère, Doucement, Austyn)
Chant sweetly every day,
And sadly, for our sin.
The bells of Osenèy
(John, Gabriel, Marie)
Chant lowly,
   Chant slowly,
Chant wistfully and holy
Of Christ, our Paladin.

Hautclère chants to the East
(His tongue is silvery high),
And Austyn like a priest
Sends west a weighty cry.
But Doucement set between
(Like an appeasive nun)
Chants cheerly,
   Chants clearly,
As if Christ heard her nearly,
A plea to every sky.

A plea that John takes up
(He is the evangelist)
Till Gabriel's angel cup
Pours sound to sun or mist.
And last of all Marie
(The virgin-voice of God)
Peals purely,
   Demurely,
And with a tone so surely
Divine, that all must hear.

The bells of Osenèy
(Doucement, Austyn, Hautclère)
Pour ever day by day
Their peals on the rapt air;
And with their mellow mates
(John, Gabriel, Marie)
Tell slowly,
        Tell lowly,
Of Christ the High and Holy,
Who makes the whole world fair.

Cale Young Rice

POETS

VAIN is the chiming of forgotten bells
    That the wind sways above a ruined shrine.
Vainer his voice in whom no longer dwells
    Hunger that craves immortal Bread and Wine.

Light songs we breathe that perish with our breath
    Out of our lips that have not kissed the rod.
They shall not live who have not tasted death.
    They only sing who are struck dumb by God.

Joyce Kilmer

ACCEPTANCE

I CANNOT think nor reason,
I only know he came
With hands and feet of healing
And wild heart all aflame.

With eyes that dimmed and softened
At all the things he saw,

And in his pillared singing
I read the marching Law.

I only know he loves me,
Enfolds and understands —
And oh, his heart that holds me,
And oh, his certain hands!

Willard Wattles

IN THE HOSPITAL

BECAUSE on the branch that is tapping my pane
A sun-wakened leaf-bud, uncurled,
Is bursting its rusty brown sheathing in twain,
I know there is Spring in the world.

Because through the sky-patch whose azure and white
My window frames all the day long,
A yellow-bird dips for an instant of flight,
I know there is Song.

Because even here in this Mansion of Woe
Where creep the dull hours, leaden-shod,
Compassion and Tenderness aid me, I know
There is God.

Arthur Guiterman

OVERNIGHT, A ROSE

THAT overnight a rose could come
I one time did believe,
For when the fairies live with one,
They wilfully deceive.
But now I know this perfect thing
Under the frozen sod

In cold and storm grew patiently
  Obedient to God.
My wonder grows, since knowledge came
  Old fancies to dismiss;
And courage comes. Was not the rose
  A winter doing this?
Nor did it know, the weary while,
  What color and perfume
With this completed loveliness
  Lay in that earthly tomb.
So maybe I, who cannot see
  What God wills not to show,
May, some day, bear a rose for Him
  It took my life to grow.

Caroline Giltinan

THE IDOL-MAKER PRAYS

GREAT god whom I shall carve from this gray stone
  Wherein thou liest, hid to all but me,
Grant thou that when my art hath made thee known
  And others bow, I shall not worship thee.
But, as I pray thee now, then let me pray
  Some greater god, — like thee to be conceived
Within my soul, — for strength to turn away
  From his new altar, when, that task achieved,
He, too, stands manifest. Yea, let me yearn
  From dream to grander dream! Let me not rest
Content at any goal! Still bid me spurn
  Each transient triumph on the Eternal Quest,
Abjuring godlings whom my hand hath made
For Deity, revealed, but unportrayed!

Arthur Guiterman

REVEILLÉ

WHAT sudden bugle calls us in the night
   And wakes us from a dream that we had shaped;
Flinging us sharply up against a fight
   We thought we had escaped.

It is no easy waking, and we win
   No final peace; our victories are few.
But still imperative forces pull us in
   And sweep us somehow through.

Summoned by a supreme and confident power
   That wakes our sleeping courage like a blow,
We rise, half-shaken, to the challenging hour,
   And answer it — and go.
                    Louis Untermeyer

THE BREAKING

(The Lord God speaks to a youth)

BEND now thy body to the common weight!
(But oh, that vine-clad head, those limbs of morn!
Those proud young shoulders I myself made straight!
How shall ye wear the yoke that must be worn?)

Look thou, my son, what wisdom comes to thee!
(But oh, that singing mouth, those radiant eyes!
Those dancing feet — that I myself made free!
How shall I sadden them to make them wise?)

Nay then, thou shalt! Resist not, have a care!
(Yea, I must work my plans who sovereign sit!
Yet do not tremble so! I cannot bear —
Though I am God — to see thee so submit!)
Margaret Steele Anderson

THE FALCONER OF GOD

I FLUNG my soul to the air like a falcon flying.
I said, "Wait on, wait on, while I ride below!
    I shall start a heron soon
    In the marsh beneath the moon —
A strange white heron rising with silver on its wings,
      Rising and crying
    Wordless, wondrous things;
The secret of the stars, of the world's heart-strings,
    The answer to their woe.
Then stoop thou upon him, and grip and hold him
    so!"

    My wild soul waited on as falcons hover.
I beat the reedy fens as I trampled past.
    I heard the mournful loon
    In the marsh beneath the moon.
And then — with feathery thunder — the bird of my
    desire
      Broke from the cover
    Flashing silver fire.
High up among the stars I saw his pinions spire.
    The pale clouds gazed aghast
As my falcon stoopt upon him, and gript and held
    him fast.

My soul dropt through the air — with heavenly plun-
    der? —
Gripping the dazzling bird my dreaming knew?
    Nay! but a piteous freight,
    A dark and heavy weight
Despoiled of silver plumage, its voice forever stilled, —
    All of the wonder
    Gone that ever filled
Its guise with glory. Oh, bird that I have killed,
    How brilliantly you flew
Across my rapturous vision when first I dreamed of
    you!

    Yet I fling my soul on high with new endeavor,
    And I ride the world below with a joyful mind.
    I shall start a heron soon
    In the marsh beneath the moon —
A wondrous silver heron its inner darkness fledges !
    I beat forever
    The fens and the sedges.
    The pledge is still the same — for all disastrous
    pledges,
    All hopes resigned!
My soul still flies above me for the quarry it shall find.
                     Wm. Rose Benét

DILEMMA

    WHAT though the moon should come
      With a blinding glow,
    And the stars have a game
      On the wood's edge,

A man would have to still
Cut and weed and sow,
And lay a white line
When he plants a hedge.

What though God
With a great sound of rain
Came to talk of violets
And things people do,
I would have to labor
And dig with my brain
Still to get a truth
Out of all words new.

Orrick Johns

TO A PORTRAIT OF WHISTLER IN THE BROOKLYN ART MUSEUM

WHAT waspish whim of Fate
Was this that bade you here
Hold dim, unhonored state,
No single courtier near?

Is there, of all who pass,
No choice, discerning few
To poise the ribboned glass
And gaze enwrapt on you?

Sword-soul that from its sheath
Laughed leaping to the fray,
How calmly underneath
Goes Brooklyn on her way!

Quite heedless of that smile —
   Half-devil and half-god,
Your quite unequalled style,
   The airy heights you trod.

Ah, could you from earth's breast
   Come back to take the air,
What matter here for jest
   Most exquisite and rare!

But since you may not come,
   Since silence holds you fast,
Since all your quips are dumb
   And all your laughter past —

I give you mine instead,
   And something with it too
That Brooklyn leaves unsaid —
   The world's fine homage due.

Ah, Prince, you smile again —
   "My faith, the court is small!"
I know, dear James — but then
   It's I or none at all!

            Eleanor Rogers Cox

FLAMMONDE [1]

THE man Flammonde, from God knows where,
With firm address and foreign air,
With news of nations in his talk
And something royal in his walk,
With glint of iron in his eyes,
But never doubt, nor yet surprise,

[1] Reprinted, by permission of the publishers, from *The Man against the Sky*, by Edwin Arlington Robinson. Copyright, 1916, by The Macmillan Company.

Appeared, and stayed, and held his head
As one by kings accredited.

Erect, with his alert repose
About him, and about his clothes,
He pictured all tradition hears
Of what we owe to fifty years.
IIis cleansing heritage of taste
Paraded neither want nor waste;
And what he needed for his fee
To live, he borrowed graciously.

He never told us what he was,
Or what mischance, or other cause,
Had banished him from better days
To play the Prince of Castaways.
Meanwhile he played surpassing well
A part, for most, unplayable;
In fine, one pauses, half afraid
To say for certain that he played.

For that, one may as well forego
Conviction as to yes or no;
Nor can I say just how intense
Would then have been the difference
To several, who, having striven
In vain to get what he was given,
Would see the stranger taken on
By friends not easy to be won.

Moreover, many a malcontent
He soothed and found munificent;
His courtesy beguiled and foiled
Suspicion that his years were soiled;

His mien distinguished any crowd,
His credit strengthened when he bowed;
And women, young and old, were fond
Of looking at the man Flammonde.

There was a woman in our town
On whom the fashion was to frown;
But while our talk renewed the tinge
Of a long-faded scarlet fringe,
The man Flammonde saw none of that,
And what he saw we wondered at —
That none of us, in her distress,
Could hide or find our littleness.

There was a boy that all agreed
Had shut within him the rare seed
Of learning. We could understand,
But none of us could lift a hand.
The man Flammonde appraised the youth,
And told a few of us the truth;
And thereby, for a little gold,
A flowered future was unrolled.

There were two citizens who fought
For years and years, and over nought;
They made life awkward for their friends,
And shortened their own dividends.
The man Flammonde said what was wrong
Should be made right, nor was it long
Before they were again in line,
And had each other in to dine.

And these I mention are but four
Of many out of many more.

So much for them. But what of him —
So firm in every look and limb?
What small satanic sort of kink
Was in his brain? What broken link
Withheld him from the destinies
That came so near to being his?

What was he, when we came to sift
His meaning, and to note the drift
Of incommunicable ways
That make us ponder while we praise?
Why was it that his charm revealed
Somehow the surface of a shield?
What was it that we never caught?
What was he, and what was he not?

How much it was of him we met
We cannot ever know; nor yet
Shall all he gave us quite atone
For what was his, and his alone;
Nor need we now, since he knew best,
Nourish an ethical unrest:
Rarely at once will nature give
The power to be Flammonde and live.

We cannot know how much we learn
From those who never will return,
Until a flash of unforeseen
Remembrance falls on what has been.
We've each a darkening hill to climb;
And this is why, from time to time
In Tilbury Town, we look beyond
Horizons for the man Flammonde.

Edwin Arlington Robinson

THE CHINESE NIGHTINGALE [1]

"How, how," he said. "Friend Chang," I said,
"San Francisco sleeps as the dead —
Ended license, lust and play:
Why do you iron the night away?
Your big clock speaks with a deadly sound,
With a tick and a wail till dawn comes round.
While the monster shadows glower and creep,
What can be better for man than sleep?"

"I will tell you a secret," Chang replied;
"My breast with vision is satisfied,
And I see green trees and fluttering wings,
And my deathless bird from Shanghai sings."
Then he lit five fire-crackers in a pan.
"Pop, pop," said the fire-crackers, "cra-cra-crack."
He lit a joss stick long and black.
Then the proud gray joss in the corner stirred;
On his wrist appeared a gray small bird,
And this was the song of the gray small bird:
"Where is the princess, loved forever,
Who made Chang first of the kings of men?"

And the joss in the corner stirred again;
And the carved dog, curled in his arms, awoke,
Barked forth a smoke-cloud that whirled and broke.
It piled in a maze round the ironing-place,
And there on the snowy table wide
Stood a Chinese lady of high degree,
With a scornful, witching, tea-rose face . . .

[1] Reprinted, by permission of the publishers, from *The Chinese Nightingale, and Other Poems*, by Vachel Lindsay. Copyright, 1917, by The Macmillan Company.

Yet she put away all form and pride,
And laid her glimmering veil aside
With a childlike smile for Chang and for me.

The walls fell back, night was aflower,
The table gleamed in a moonlit bower,
While Chang, with a countenance carved of stone,
Ironed and ironed, all alone.
And thus she sang to the busy man Chang:
"Have you forgotten . . .
Deep in the ages, long, long ago,
I was your sweetheart, there on the sand —
Storm-worn beach of the Chinese land?
We sold our grain in the peacock town
Built on the edge of the sea-sands brown —
Built on the edge of the sea-sands brown . . .

When all the world was drinking blood
From the skulls of men and bulls
And all the world had swords and clubs of stone,
We drank our tea in China beneath the sacred spice-
        trees,
And heard the curled waves of the harbor moan.
And this gray bird, in Love's first spring,
With a bright-bronze breast and a bronze-brown wing,
Captured the world with his carolling.
Do you remember, ages after,
At last the world we were born to own?
You were the heir of the yellow throne —
The world was the field of the Chinese man
And we were the pride of the Sons of Han?
We copied deep books and we carved in jade,
And wove blue silks in the mulberry shade . . ."

"I remember, I remember
That Spring came on forever,
That Spring came on forever,"
Said the Chinese nightingale.

My heart was filled with marvel and dream,
Though I saw the western street-lamps gleam,
Though dawn was bringing the western day,
Though Chang was a laundryman ironing away ...
Mingled there with the streets and alleys,
The railroad-yard and the clock-tower bright,
Demon clouds crossed ancient valleys;
Across wide lotus-ponds of light
I marked a giant firefly's flight.

And the lady, rosy-red,
Flourished her fan, her shimmering fan,
Stretched her hand toward Chang, and said:
"Do you remember,
Ages after,
Our palace of heart-red stone?
Do you remember
The little doll-faced children
With their lanterns full of moon-fire,
That came from all the empire
Honoring the throne? —
The loveliest fête and carnival
Our world had ever known?
The sages sat about us
With their heads bowed in their beards,
With proper meditation on the sight.
Confucius was not born;
We lived in those great days

Confucius later said were lived aright . . .
And this gray bird, on that day of spring,
With a bright-bronze breast, and a bronze-brown
     wing,
Captured the world with his carolling.
Late at night his tune was spent.
Peasants,
Sages,
Children,
Homeward went,
And then the bronze bird sang for you and me.
We walked alone. Our hearts were high and free.
I had a silvery name, I had a silvery name,
I had a silvery name — do you remember
The name you cried beside the tumbling sea?"

Chang turned not to the lady slim —
He bent to his work, ironing away;
But she was arch, and knowing and glowing,
And the bird on his shoulder spoke for him.

"Darling . . . darling . . . darling . . . darling . . . "
Said the Chinese nightingale.

The great gray joss on a rustic shelf,
Rakish and shrewd, with his collar awry,
Sang impolitely, as though by himself,
Drowning with his bellowing the nightingale's cry:
"Back through a hundred, hundred years
Hear the waves as they climb the piers,
Hear the howl of the silver seas,
Hear the thunder.
Hear the gongs of holy China

How the waves and tunes combine
In a rhythmic clashing wonder,
Incantation old and fine:
        'Dragons, dragons, Chinese dragons,
        Red fire-crackers, and green fire-crackers,
        And dragons, dragons, Chinese dragons.' "

Then the lady, rosy-red,
Turned to her lover Chang and said:
"Dare you forget that turquoise dawn,
When we stood in our mist-hung velvet lawn,
And worked a spell this great joss taught
Till a God of the Dragons was charmed and caught?
From the flag high over our palace home
He flew to our feet in rainbow-foam —
A king of beauty and tempest and thunder
Panting to tear our sorrows asunder:
A dragon of fair adventure and wonder.
We mounted the back of that royal slave
With thoughts of desire that were noble and grave.
We swam down the shore to the dragon-mountains,
We whirled to the peaks and the fiery fountains.
To our secret ivory house we were borne.
We looked down the wonderful wing-filled regions
Where the dragons darted in glimmering legions.
Right by my breast the nightingale sang;
The old rhymes rang in the sunlit mist
That we this hour regain —
Song-fire for the brain.
When my hands and my hair and my feet you kissed,
When you cried for your heart's new pain,
What was my name in the dragon-mist,
In the rings of rainbowed rain?"

"Sorrow and love, glory and love,"
Said the Chinese nightingale.
"Sorrow and love, glory and love,"
Said the Chinese nightingale.

And now the joss broke in with his song:
"Dying ember, bird of Chang,
Soul of Chang, do you remember? —
Ere you returned to the shining harbor
There were pirates by ten thousand
Descended on the town
In vessels mountain-high and red and brown,
Moon-ships that climbed the storms and cut the
          skies.
On their prows were painted terrible bright eyes.
But I was then a wizard and a scholar and a
          priest;
I stood upon the sand;
With lifted hand I looked upon them
And sunk their vessels with my wizard eyes,
And the stately lacquer-gate made safe again.
Deep, deep below the bay, the sea-weed and the
          spray,
Embalmed in amber every pirate lies,
Embalmed in amber every pirate lies."

Then this did the noble lady say:
"Bird, do you dream of our home-coming day
When you flew like a courier on before
From the dragon-peak to our palace-door,
And we drove the steed in your singing path —
The ramping dragon of laughter and wrath:
And found our city all aglow,

And knighted this joss that decked it so?
There were golden fishes in the purple river
And silver fishes and rainbow fishes.
There were golden junks in the laughing river.
And silver junks and rainbow junks:
There were golden lilies by the bay and river,
And silver lilies and tiger-lilies,
And tinkling wind-bells in the gardens of the
      town
By the black-lacquer gate
Where walked in state
The kind king Chang
And his sweetheart mate . . .
With his flag-born dragon
And his crown of pearl . . . and . . . jade,
And his nightingale reigning in the mulberry
      shade,
And sailors and soldiers on the sea-sands brown,
And priests who bowed them down to your song —
By the city called Han, the peacock town,
By the city called Han, the nightingale town,
The nightingale town."

Then sang the bird, so strangely gay,
Fluttering, fluttering, ghostly and gray,
A vague, unravelling, final tune,
Like a long unwinding silk cocoon;
Sang as though for the soul of him
Who ironed away in that bower dim: —
    "I have forgotten
    Your dragons great,
    Merry and mad and friendly and bold.
    Dim is your proud lost palace-gate.

I vaguely know
There were heroes of old,
Troubles more than the heart could hold,
There were wolves in the woods
Yet lambs in the fold,
Nests in the top of the almond tree . . .
The evergreen tree . . . and the mulberry
          ·tree . . .
Life and hurry and joy forgotten,
Years on years I but half-remember . . .
Man is a torch, then ashes soon,
May and June, then dead December,
Dead December, then again June.
Who shall end my dream's confusion?
Life is a loom, weaving illusion . . .
I remember, I remember
There were ghostly veils and laces . . .
In the shadowy bowery places . . .
With lovers' ardent faces
Bending to one another,
Speaking each his part.
They infinitely echo
In the red cave of my heart.
'Sweetheart, sweetheart, sweetheart,'
They said to one another.
They spoke, I think, of perils past.
They spoke, I think, of peace at last.
One thing I remember:
Spring came on forever,
Spring came on forever,"
Said the Chinese nightingale.

Vachel Lindsay

LOVE SONGS

COME [1]

COME, when the pale moon like a petal
  Floats in the pearly dusk of Spring,
Come with arms outstretched to take me,
  Come with lips that long to cling.

Come, for life is a frail moth flying,
  Caught in the web of the years that pass,
And soon we two, so warm and eager,
  Will be as the gray stones in the grass.

MESSAGE [1]

I HEARD a cry in the night,
  A thousand miles it came,
Sharp as a flash of light,
  My name, my name!

It was your voice I heard,
  You waked and loved me so —
I send you back this word,
  I know, I know!

MOODS [1]

I AM the still rain falling,
  Too tired for singing mirth —
Oh, be the green fields calling,
  Oh, be for me the earth!

[1] Reprinted, by permission of the publishers, from *Love Songs*, by Sara Teasdale. Copyright, 1917, by The Macmillan Company.

I am the brown bird pining
　To leave the nest and fly —
Oh, be the fresh cloud shining,
　Oh, be for me the sky!

NIGHT SONG AT AMALFI [1]

I ASKED the heaven of stars
　What I should give my love —
It answered me with silence,
　Silence above.

I asked the darkened sea
　Down where the fishers go —
It answered me with silence,
　Silence below.

Oh, I could give him weeping,
　Or I could give him song —
But how can I give silence
　My whole life long?

SONG

LET it be forgotten as a flower is forgotten,
　Forgotten as a fire that once was singing gold,
Let it be forgotten forever and ever,
　Time is a kind friend, he will make us old.

If any one asks, say it was forgotten
　Long and long ago,
As a flower, as a fire, as a hushed footfall
　In a long forgotten snow.

Sara Teasdale

[1] Reprinted, by permission of the publishers, from *Love Songs*, by Sara Teasdale. Copyright, 1917, by the Macmillan Company.

LOVE IS A TERRIBLE THING

I WENT out to the farthest meadow,
I lay down in the deepest shadow;

And I said unto the earth, "Hold me,"
And unto the night, "O enfold me,"

And unto the wind petulantly
I cried, "You know not for you are free!"

And I begged the little leaves to lean
Low and together for a safe screen;

Then to the stars I told my tale:
"That is my home-light, there in the vale,

"And O, I know that I shall return,
But let me lie first mid the unfeeling fern.

"For there is a flame that has blown too near,
And there is a name that has grown too dear,
And there is a fear . . . "

And to the still hills and cool earth and far
    sky I made moan,
"The heart in my bosom is not my own!

"O would I were free as the wind on wing;
Love is a terrible thing!"

Grace Fallow Norton

VALLEY SONG

YOUR eyes and the valley are memories.
Your eyes fire and the valley a bowl.
It was here a moonrise crept over the timberline.
It was here we turned the coffee cups upside down.
And your eyes and the moon swept the valley.

I will see you again to-morrow.
I will see you again in`a million years.
I will never know your dark eyes again.
These are three ghosts I keep.
These are three sumach-red dogs I run with.

All of it wraps and knots to a riddle:
I have the moon, the timberline, and you.
All three are gone — and I keep all three.

Carl Sandburg

SPRING IN CARMEL

O'ER Carmel fields in the springtime the sea-gulls
    follow the plow.
  White, white wings on the blue above!
  White were your brow and breast, O Love!
    But I cannot see you now.
  Tireless ever the Mission swallow
  Dips to meadow and poppied hollow;
  Well for her mate that he can follow,
    As the buds are on the bough.

By the woods and waters of Carmel the lark is glad
    in the sun.
  Harrow! Harrow! Music of God!

Near to your nest her feet have trod
   Whose journeyings are done.
Sing, O lover! I cannot sing.
Wild and sad are the thoughts you bring.
Well for you are the skies of spring,
   And to me all skies are one.

In the beautiful woods of Carmel an iris bends
     to the wind.
O thou far-off and sorrowful flower!
Rose that I found in a tragic hour!
   Rose that I shall not find!
Petals that fell so soft and slowly,
Fragrant snows on the grasses lowly,
Gathered now would I call you holy
   Ever to eyes once blind.

In the pine-sweet valley of Carmel the cream-
     cups scatter in foam.
Azures of early lupin there!
Now the wild lilac floods the air
   Like a broken honey-comb.
So could the flowers of Paradise
Pour their souls to the morning skies;
So like a ghost your fragrance lies
   On the path that once led home.

On the emerald hills of Carmel the spring and
     winter have met.
   Here I find in a gentled spot
   The frost of the wild forget-me-not,
     And — I cannot forget.

Heart once light as the floating feather
Borne aloft in the sunny weather,
Spring and winter have come together —
  Shall you and she meet yet?

On the rocks and beaches of Carmel the surf is
  mighty to-day.
Breaker and lifting billow call
To the high, blue Silence over all
  With the word no heart can say.
Time-to-be, shall I hear it ever?
Time-that-is, with the hands that sever,
Cry all words but the dreadful "Never"!
  And name of her far away.

George Sterling

MUSIC I HEARD

Music I heard with you was more than music,
And bread I broke with you was more than bread;
Now that I am without you, all is desolate;
All that was once so beautiful is dead.

Your hands once touched this table and this silver,
And I have seen your fingers hold this glass.
These things do not remember you, belovèd, —
And yet your touch upon them will not pass.

For it was in my heart you moved among them,
And blessed them with your hands and with your eyes;
And in my heart they will remember always, —
They knew you once, O beautiful and wise.

Conrad Aiken

DUSK AT SEA

To-night eternity alone is near:
  The sea, the sunset, and the darkening blue;
Within their shelter is no space for fear,
  Only the wonder that such things are true.

The thought of you is like the dusk at sea —
  Space and wide freedom and old shores left far,
The shelter of a lone immensity
  Sealed by the sunset and the evening star.

Thomas S. Jones, Jr.

OLD SHIPS

There is a memory stays upon old ships,
  A weightless cargo in the musty hold, —
Of bright lagoons and prow-caressing lips,
  Of stormy midnights, — and a tale untold.
They have remembered islands in the dawn,
  And windy capes that tried their slender spars,
And tortuous channels where their keels have gone,
  And calm blue nights of stillness and the stars.

Ah, never think that ships forget a shore,
  Or bitter seas, or winds that made them wise;
There is a dream upon them, evermore; —
  And there be some who say that sunk ships rise
To seek familiar harbors in the night,
  Blowing in mists, their spectral sails like light.

David Morton

THE WANDERER

THE ships are lying in the bay,
  The gulls are swinging round their spars;
My soul as eagerly as they
  Desires the margin of the stars.

So much do I love wandering,
  So much I love the sea and sky,
That it will be a piteous thing
  In one small grave to lie.

Zoë Akins

HARBURY

ALL the men of Harbury go down to the sea in ships,
The wind upon their faces, the salt upon their lips.

The little boys of Harbury when they are laid to
    sleep,
Dream of masts and cabins and the wonders of the
    deep.

The women-folk of Harbury have eyes like the sea,
Wide with watching wonder, deep with mystery.

I met a woman: "Beyond the bar," she said,
"Beyond the shallow water where the green lines
    spread,

"Out beyond the sand-bar and the white spray,
My three sons wait for the Judgment Day."

I saw an old man who goes to sea no more,
Watch from morn till evening down on the shore.

"The sea's a hard mistress," the old man said;
"The sea is always hungry and never full fed.

"The sea had my father and took my son from me —
Sometimes I think I see them, walking on the sea!

"I'd like to be in Harbury on the Judgment Day,
When the word is spoken and the sea is wiped away,

"And all the drowned fisher boys, with sea-weed in
      their hair,
Rise and walk to Harbury to greet the women there.

"I'd like to be in Harbury to see the souls arise,
Son and mother hand in hand, lovers with glad eyes.

"I think there would be many who would turn and
      look with me,
Hoping for another glimpse of the cruel sea!

"They tell me that in Paradise the fields are green and
      still,
With pleasant flowers everywhere that all may take
      who will,

"And four great rivers flowing from out the Throne
      of God
That no one ever drowns in and souls may cross dry-
      shod.

"I think among those wonders there will be men like
    me,
Who miss the old salt danger of the singing sea.

"For in my heart, like some old shell, inland, safe and
    dry,
Any one who harks will still hear the sea cry."
                           Louise Driscoll

A LYNMOUTH WIDOW

He was straight and strong, and his eyes were blue
As the summer meeting of sky and sea,
And the ruddy cliffs had a colder hue
Than flushed his cheek when he married me.

We passed the porch where the swallows breed,
We left the little brown church behind,
And I leaned on his arm, though I had no need,
Only to feel him so strong and kind.

One thing I never can quite forget;
It grips my throat when I try to pray —
The keen salt smell of a drying net
That hung on the churchyard wall that day.

He would have taken a long, long grave —
A long, long grave, for he stood so tall . . .
Oh, God, the crash of a breaking wave,
And the smell of the nets on the churchyard wall!
                      Amelia Josephine Burr

CITY ROOFS

ROOF-TOPS, roof-tops, what do you cover?
Sad folk, bad folk, and many a glowing lover;
Wise people, simple people, children of despair —
Roof-tops, roof-tops, hiding pain and care.

Roof-tops, roof-tops, O what sin you're knowing,
While above you in the sky the white clouds are
      blowing;
While beneath you, agony and dolor and grim strife
Fight the olden battle, the olden war of Life.

Roof-tops, roof-tops, cover up their shame —
Wretched souls, prisoned souls too piteous to name;
Man himself hath built you all to hide away the
      stars —
Roof-tops roof-tops, you hide ten million scars.

Roof-tops, roof-tops, well I know you cover
Many solemn tragedies and many a lonely lover;
But ah, you hide the good that lives in the throbbing
      city —
Patient wives, and tenderness, forgiveness, faith, and
      pity.

Roof-tops, roof-tops, this is what I wonder:
You are thick as poisonous plants, thick the people
      under;
Yet roofless, and homeless, and shelterless they roam,
The driftwood of the town who have no roof-top and
      no home!

Charles Hanson Towne

EYE-WITNESS

Down by the railroad in a green valley
By dancing water, there he stayed awhile
Singing, and three men with him, listeners,
All tramps, all homeless reapers of the wind,
Motionless now and while the song went on
Transfigured into mages thronged with visions;
There with the late light of the sunset on them
And on clear water spinning from a spring
Through little cones of sand dancing and fading,
Close beside pine woods where a hermit thrush
Cast, when love dazzled him, shadows of music
That lengthened, fluting, through the singer's pauses
While the sure earth rolled eastward bringing stars
Over the singer and the men that listened
There by the roadside, understanding all.

A train went by but nothing seemed to be changed.
Some eye at a car window must have flashed
From the plush world inside the glassy Pullman,
Carelessly bearing off the scene forever,
With idle wonder what the men were doing,
Seeing they were so strangely fixed and seeing
Torn papers from their smeary dreary meal
Spread on the ground with old tomato cans
Muddy with dregs of lukewarm chicory,
Neglected while they listened to the song.
And while he sang the singer's face was lifted,
And the sky shook down a soft light upon him
Out of its branches where like fruits there were
Many beautiful stars and planets moving,
With lands upon them, rising from their seas,

Glorious lands with glittering sands upon them,
With soils of gold and magic mould for seeding,
The shining loam of lands afoam with gardens
On mightier stars with giant rains and suns
There in the heavens; but on none of all
Was there ground better than he stood upon:
There was no world there in the sky above him
Deeper in promise than the earth beneath him
Whose dust had flowered up in him the singer
And three men understanding every word.

The Tramp Sings:

I will sing, I will go, and never ask me "Why?"
I was born a rover and a passer-by.

I seem to myself like water and sky,
A river and a rover and a passer-by.

But in the winter three years back
We lit us a night fire by the track,

And the snow came up and the fire it flew
And we could n't find the warming room for two.

One had to suffer, so I left him the fire
And I went to the weather from my heart's desire.

It was night on the line, it was no more fire,
But the zero whistle through the icy wire.

As I went suffering through the snow
Something like a shadow came moving slow.

I went up to it and I said a word;
Something flew above it like a kind of bird.

I leaned in closer and I saw a face;
A light went round me but I kept my place.

My heart went open like an apple sliced;
I saw my Saviour and I saw my Christ.

Well, you may not read it in a book,
But it takes a gentle Saviour to give a gentle look.

I looked in his eyes and I read the news;
His heart was having the railroad blues.

Oh, the railroad blues will cost you dear,
Keeps you moving on for something that you
        don't see here.

We stood and whispered in a kind of moon;
The line was looking like May and June.

I found he was a roamer and a journey man
Looking for a lodging since the night began.

He went to the doors but he did n't have the pay.
He went to the windows, then he went away.

Says, "We'll walk together and we'll both be fed."
Says, "I will give you the 'other' bread."

Oh, the bread he gave and without money!
O drink, O fire, O burning honey!

It went all through me like a shining storm.
I saw inside me, it was light and warm.

I saw deep under and I saw above,
I saw the stars weighed down with love.

They sang that love to burning birth,
They poured that music to the earth.

I heard the stars sing low like mothers.
He said: "Now look, and help feed others."

I looked around, and as close as touch
Was everybody that suffered much.

They reached out, there was darkness only;
They could not see us, they were lonely.

I saw the hearts that deaths took hold of,
With the wounds bare that were not told of;

Hearts with things in them making gashes;
Hearts that were choked with their dreams' ashes;

Women in front of the rolled-back air,
Looking at their breasts and nothing there;

Good men wasting and trapped in hells;
Hurt lads shivering with the fare-thee-wells.

I saw them as if something bound them;
I stood there but my heart went round them.

I begged him not to let me see them wasted.
Says, "Tell them then what you have tasted."

Told him I was weak as a rained-on bee;
Told him I was lost. — Says: "Lean on me."

Something happened then I could not tell,
But I knew I had the water for every hell.

Any other thing it was no use bringing;
They needed what the stars were singing,

What the whole sky sang like waves of light,
The tune that it danced to, day and night.

Oh, I listened to the sky for the tune to come;
The song seemed easy, but I stood there dumb.

The stars could feel me reaching through them
They let down light and drew me to them.

I stood in the sky in a light like day,
Drinking in the word that all things say

Where the worlds hang growing in clustered shapes
Dripping the music like wine from grapes.

With "Love, Love, Love," above the pain,
— The vine-like song with its wine-like rain.

Through heaven under heaven the song takes root
Of the turning, burning, deathless fruit.

I came to the earth and the pain so near me,
I tried that song but they could n't hear me.

I went down into the ground to grow,
A seed for a song that would make men know.

Into the ground from my roamer's light
I went; he watched me sink to night.

Deep in the ground from my human grieving,
His pain ploughed in me to believing.

Oh, he took earth's pain to be his bride,
While the heart of life sang in his side.

For I felt that pain, I took its kiss,
My heart broke into dust with his.

Then sudden through the earth I found life springing:
The dust men trampled on was singing.

Deep in my dust I felt its tones;
The roots of beauty went round my bones.

I stirred, I rose like a flame, like a river,
I stood on the line, I could sing forever.

Love had pierced into my human sheathing,
Song came out of me simple as breathing.

A freight came by, the line grew colder,
He laid his hand upon my shoulder.

Says, "Don't stay on the line such nights,"
And led me by the hand to the station lights.

I asked him in front of the station-house wall
If he had lodging. Says, "None at all."

I pointed to my heart and looked in his face. —
"Here, — if you have n't got a better place."

He looked and he said: "Oh, we still must roam
But if you 'll keep it open, well, I 'll call it 'home.'"

The thrush now slept whose pillow was his wing.
So the song ended and the four remained
Still in the faint starshine that silvered them,
While the low sound went on of broken water
Out of the spring and through the darkness flowing
Over a stone that held it from the sea.
Whether the men spoke after could not be told,
A mist from the ground so veiled them, but they waited
A little longer till the moon came up;
Then on the gilded track leading to the mountains,
Against the moon they faded in common gold
And earth bore East with all toward the new morning.

Ridgely Torrence

GOD'S ACRE

BECAUSE we felt there could not be
A mowing in reality
So white and feathery-blown and gay
With blossoms of wild caraway,
I said to Celia, "Let us trace
The secret of this pleasant place!"

We knew some deeper beauty lay
Below the bloom of caraway,
And when we bent the white aside
We came to paupers who had died:
Rough wooden shingles row on row,
And God's name written there — *John Doe.*
Witter Bynner

GENERAL WILLIAM BOOTH ENTERS INTO HEAVEN [1]

(To be sung to the tune of *The Blood of the Lamb* with indicated instrument)

I

(Bass drum beaten loudly)

BOOTH led boldly with his big bass drum —
(Are you washed in the blood of the Lamb?)
The Saints smiled gravely and they said: "He's come."
(Are you washed in the blood of the Lamb?)
Walking lepers followed, rank on rank,
Lurching bravoes from the ditches dank,
Drabs from the alleyways and drug fiends pale —
Minds still passion-ridden, soul-powers frail: —
Vermin-eaten saints with mouldy breath,
Unwashed legions with the ways of Death —
(Are you washed in the blood of the Lamb?)

(Banjos)

Every slum had sent its half-a-score
The round world over. (Booth had groaned for more.)
Every banner that the wide world flies
Bloomed with glory and transcendent dyes.

[1] Reprinted, by permission of the publishers, from *General William Booth Enters into Heaven, and Other Poems,* by Vachel Lindsay. Copyright, 1913, by The Macmillan Company.

Big-voiced lasses made their banjos bang,
Tranced, fanatical, they shrieked and sang: —
"Are you washed in the blood of the Lamb?"
Hallelujah! It was queer to see
Bull-necked convicts with that land make free.
Loons with trumpets blowed a blare, blare, blare,
On, on upward thro' the golden air!
(Are you washed in the blood of the Lamb?)

II
(Bass drum slower and softer)

Booth died blind and still by Faith he trod,
Eyes still dazzled by the ways of God.
Booth led boldly, and he looked the chief,
Eagle countenance in sharp relief,
Beard a-flying, air of high command
Unabated in that holy land.

(Sweet flute music)

Jesus came from out the court-house door,
Stretched his hands above the passing poor.
Booth saw not, but led his queer ones there
Round and round the mighty court-house square.
Yet in an instant all that blear review
Marched on spotless, clad in raiment new.
The lame were straightened, withered limbs uncurled
And blind eyes opened on a new, sweet world.

(Bass drum louder)

Drabs and vixens in a flash made whole!
Gone was the weasel-head, the snout, the jowl!
Sages and sibyls now, and athletes clean,
Rulers of empires and of forests green!

*(Grand chorus of all instruments. Tambourines to the
foreground)*

The hosts were sandalled, and their wings were
    fire!
(Are you washed in the blood of the Lamb?)
But their noise played havoc with the angel-choir
(Are you washed in the blood of the Lamb?)
O, shout Salvation! It was good to see
Kings and Princes by the Lamb set free.
The banjos rattled and the tambourines
Jing-jing-jingled in the hands of Queens.

(Reverently sung, no instruments)

And when Booth halted by the curb for prayer
He saw his Master thro' the flag-filled air.
Christ came gently with a robe and crown
For Booth the soldier, while the throng knelt down.
He saw King Jesus. They were face to face,
And he knelt a-weeping in that holy place.
Are you washed in the blood of the Lamb?

                      Vachel Lindsay

COMPENSATION

I KNOW the sorrows of the last abyss:
I walked the cold black pools without a star;
I lay on rock of unseen flint and spar;
I heard the execrable serpent hiss;
I dreamed of sun, fruit-tree, and virgin's kiss;
I woke alone with midnight near and far,
And everlasting hunger, keen to mar;
But I arose, and my reward is this:

I am no more one more amid the throng: ·
Though name be naught, and lips forever weak,
I seem to know at last of mighty song;
And with no blush, no tremor on the cheek,
I do claim consort with the great and strong
Who suffered ill and had the gift to speak.

William Ellery Leonard

A GIRL'S SONGS

BORROWER

I SING of sorrow,
    I sing of weeping.
I have no sorrow.

I only borrow
From some tomorrow
    Where it lies sleeping,
Enough of sorrow
    To sing of weeping.

VINTAGE

Heartbreak that is too new
    Can not be used to make
Beauty that will startle;
    That takes an old heartbreak.

Old heartbreaks are old wine.
Too new to pour is mine.

THE KISS

Your kiss lies on my face
    Like the first snow
Upon a summer place.

Bewildered by that wonder,
The grasses tremble under
The thing they do not know.
I tremble even so.

FREE

Over and over
   I tell the sky:
   I am free — I!

Over and over I tell the sea:
   — I am free!

Over and over I tell my lover
   I am free, free!
Over and over.

But when the night comes black and cold,
I who am young, with fear grow old;
And I know, when the world is clear of sound,
I am bound — bound.

                  Mary Carolyn Davies

THE ENCHANTED SHEEPFOLD

THE hills far-off were blue, blue,
   The hills at hand were brown;
And all the herd-bells called to me
   As I came by the down.

The briars turned to roses, roses;
   Ever we stayed to pull

, A white little rose, and a red little rose,
    And a lock of silver wool.

Nobody heeded,— none, none;
    And when True Love came by,
They thought him naught but the shepherd-boy.
    Nobody knew but I!

The trees were feathered like birds, birds;
    Birds were in every tree.
Yet nobody heeded, nobody heard,
    Nobody knew, save me.

And he is fairer than all — all.
    How could a heart go wrong?
For his eyes I knew, and his knew mine,
    Like an old, old song.

Josephine Preston Peabody

WHERE LOVE IS

By the rosy cliffs of Devon, on a green hill's crest,
I would build me a house as a swallow builds its nest;
I would curtain it with roses, and the wind should
        breathe to me
The sweetness of the roses and the saltness of the sea.

Where the Tuscan olives whiten in the hot blue day,
I would hide me from the heat in a little hut of gray,
While the singing of the husbandman should scale my
        lattice green
From the golden rows of barley that the poppies blaze
        between.

Narrow is the street, Dear, and dingy are the walls
Wherein I wait your coming as the twilight falls.
All day with dreams I gild the grime till at your step
    I start —
Ah Love, my country in your arms — my home upon
    your heart!

                      Amelia Josephine Burr

INTERLUDE [1]

I AM not old, but old enough
To know that you are very young.
It might be said I am the leaf,
And you the blossom newly sprung.

So I shall grow a while with you,
And hear the bee and watch the cloud,
Before the dragon on the branch,
The caterpillar, weaves a shroud.

                      Scudder Middleton

THE LOVER ENVIES AN OLD MAN

I ENVY the feeble old man
Dozing there in the sun.
When all you can do is done
And life is a shattered plan,
What is there better than
Dozing in the sun?

I could grow very still
Like an old stone on a hill

[1] Reprinted, by permission of the publishers, from *The New Day*, by Scudder Middleton. Copyright, 1919, by The Macmillan Company.

And content me with the one
Thing that is ever kind,
The tender sun.
I could grow deaf and blind
And never hear her voice,
Nor think I could rejoice
With her in any place;
And I could forget her face,
And love only the sun.
Because when we are tired,
Very very tired,
And cannot again be fired
By any hope,
The sun is so comforting!
A little bird under the wing
Of its mother, is not so warm.
Give me only the scope
Of an old chair
Out in the air,
Let me rest there,
Moving not,
Loving not,
Only dozing my days till my days be done,
Under the sun.

Shaemas O Sheel

IF YOU SHOULD TIRE OF LOVING ME

IF you should tire of loving me
   Some one of our far days,
Oh, never start to hide your heart
   Or cover thought with praise.

For every word you would not say
Be sure my heart has heard,
So go from me all silently
Without a kiss or word;

For God must give you happiness,
And Oh, it may befall
In listening long to Heaven-song
I may not care at all!

Margaret Widdemer

THE FLOWER OF MENDING [1]

WHEN Dragon-fly would fix his wings,
When Snail would patch his house,
When moths have marred the overcoat
Of tender Mister Mouse,

The pretty creatures go with haste
To the sunlit blue-grass hills
Where the Flower of Mending yields the wax
And webs to help their ills.

The hour the coats are waxed and webbed
They fall into a dream,
And when they wake the ragged robes
Are joined without a seam.

My heart is but a dragon-fly,
My heart is but a mouse,
My heart is but a haughty snail
In a little stony house.

[1] Reprinted, by permission of the publishers, from *The Chinese Nightingale, and Other Poems*, by Vachel Lindsay. Copyright, 1917, by The Macmillan Company.

Your hand was honey-comb to heal,
Your voice a web to bind.
You were a Mending Flower to me
To cure my heart and mind.

Vachel Lindsay

VENUS TRANSIENS[1]

TELL me,
Was Venus more beautiful
Than you are,
When she topped
The crinkled waves,
Drifting shoreward
On her plaited shell?
Was Botticelli's vision
Fairer than mine;
And were the painted rosebuds
He tossed his lady,
Of better worth
Than the words I blow about you
To cover your too great loveliness
As with a gauze
Of misted silver?

For me,
You stand poised
In the blue and buoyant air,
Cinctured by bright winds,
Treading the sunlight.
And the waves which precede you
Ripple and stir
The sands at your feet.

Amy Lowell

1 Reprinted, by permission of the publishers, from *Pictures of the Floating World*, by Amy Lowell. Copyright. 1919, by The Macmillan Company.

THE DREAM OF AENGUS OG

WHEN the rose of Morn through the Dawn was breaking,
  And white on the hearth was last night's flame,
Thither to me 'twixt sleeping and waking,
  Singing out of the mists she came.

And grey as the mists on the spectre meadows
  Were the eyes that on my eyes she laid,
And her hair's red splendor through the shadows
  Like to the marsh-fire gleamed and played.

And she sang of the wondrous far-off places
  That a man may only see in dreams,
The death-still, odorous, starlit spaces
  Where Time is lost and no life gleams.

And there till the day had its crest uplifted,
  She stood with her still face bent on me,
Then forth with the Dawn departing drifted
  Light as a foam-fleck on the sea.

And now my heart is the heart of a swallow
  That here no solace of rest may find,
Forevermore I follow and follow
  Her white feet glancing down the wind.

And forevermore in my ears are ringing —
  (Oh, red lips yet shall I kiss you dumb!)
Twain sole words of that May morn's singing,
  Calling to me "Hither"! and "Come"!

From flower-bright fields to the wild lake-sedges
  Crying my steps when the Day has gone,

Till dim and small down the Night's pale edges
  The stars have fluttered one by one.

And light as the thought of a love forgotten,
  The hours skim past, while before me flies
That face of the Sun and Mist begotten,
  Its singing lips and death-cold eyes.
                    Eleanor Rogers Cox

"I AM IN LOVE WITH HIGH FAR-SEEING PLACES"

I AM in love with high far-seeing places
That look on plains half-sunlight and half-storm, —
In love with hours when from the circling faces
Veils pass, and laughing fellowship glows warm.
You who look on me with grave eyes where rapture
And April love of living burn confessed,—
The Gods are good! The world lies free to capture!
Life has no walls. O take me to your breast!
Take me, — be with me for a moment's span! —
I am in love with all unveilèd faces.
I seek the wonder at the heart of man;
I would go up to the far-seeing places.
While youth is ours, turn toward me for a space
The marvel of your rapture-lighted face!
                    Arthur Davison Ficke

YOU

    DEEP in the heart of me,
    Nothing but You!
    See through the art of me —
    Deep in the heart of me

Find the best part of me,
Changeless and true.
Deep in the heart of me,
Nothing but You!

Ruth Guthrie Harding

CHOICE

I'd rather have the thought of you
To hold against my heart,
My spirit to be taught of you
With west winds blowing,
Than all the warm caresses
Of another love's bestowing,
Or all the glories of the world
In which you had no part.

I'd rather have the theme of you
To thread my nights and days,
I'd rather have the dream of you
With faint stars glowing,
I'd rather have the want of you,
The rich, elusive taunt of you
Forever and forever and forever unconfessed
Than claim the alien comfort
Of any other's breast.

O lover! O my lover,
That this should come to me!
I'd rather have the hope for you,
Ah, Love, I'd rather grope for you
Within the great abyss
Than claim another's kiss —

Alone I'd rather go my way
Throughout eternity.

Angela Morgan

SONG

THE bride, she wears a white, white rose — the
    plucking it was mine;
The poet wears a laurel wreath — and I the laurel
    twine;
And oh, the child, your little child, that's clinging
    close to you,
It laughs to wear my violets — they are so sweet and
    blue!

And I, I have a wreath to wear — ah, never rue nor
    thorn!
I sometimes think that bitter wreath could be more
    sweetly worn!
For mine is made of ghostly bloom, of what I can't
    forget —
The fallen leaves of other crowns — rose, laurel,
    violet!

Margaret Steele Anderson

ROMANCE [1]

WHY should we argue with the falling dust
Or tremble in the traffic of the days?
Our hearts are music-makers in the clouds,
Our feet are running on the heavenly ways.

[1] Reprinted, by permission of the publishers, from *The New Day*, by
Scudder Middleton. Copyright, 1919, by The Macmillan Company.

We'll go and find the honey of romance
Within the hollow of the sacred tree.
There is a spirit in the eastern sky,
Calling along the dawn to you and me.

She'll lead us to the forest where she hides
The yellow wine that keeps the angels young —
We are the chosen lovers of the earth
For whom alone the golden comb was hung.

Scudder Middleton

GOOD-BYE

GOOD-BYE to tree and tower,
To meadow, stream, and hill,
Beneath the white clouds marshalled close
At the wind's will.

Good-bye to the gay garden,
With prim geraniums pied,
And spreading yew trees, old, unchanging
Tho' men have died.

Good-bye to the New Castle,
With granite walls and grey,
And rooms where faded greatness still
Lingers to-day.

To every friend in Mallow,
When I am gone afar,
These words of ancient Celtic hope,
"Peace after war."

I would return to Erin
When all these wars are by,
Live long among her hills before
My last good-bye.

Norreys Jephson O'Conor

BEYOND RATHKELLY

As I went over the Far Hill,
    Just beyond Rathkelly,
    — Och, to be on the Far Hill
O'er Newtonstewart Town!
As I went over the Far Hill
    With Marget's daughter Nellie,
The night was up and the moon was out,
    And a star was falling down.

As I went over the Far Hill,
    Just beyond Rathkelly,
    — Och, to be on the Far Hill
Above the Bridge o'Moyle!
As I went over the Far Hill,
    With Marget's daughter Nellie,
I made a wish before the star
    Had fallen in the Foyle.

As I went over the Far Hill,
    Just beyond Rathkelly,
    — Och, to be on the Far Hill
With the hopes that I had then!
As I went over the Far Hill,
    I wished for little Nellie,
And if a star were falling now
    I'd wish for her again.

Francis Carlin

A SONG OF TWO WANDERERS

DEAR, when I went with you
To where the town ends,
Simple things that Christ loved —
They were our friends;
Tree shade and grass blade
And meadows in flower;
Sun-sparkle, dew-glisten,
Star-glow and shower;
Cool-flowing song at night
Where the river bends,
And the shingle croons a tune —
These were our friends.

Under us the brown earth
Ancient and strong,
The best bed for wanderers
All the night long;
Over us the blue sky
Ancient and dear,
The best roof to shelter all
Glad wanderers here;
And racing between them there
Falls and ascends
The chantey of the clean winds —
These were our friends.

By day on the broad road
Or on the narrow trail,
Angel wings shadowed us,
Glimmering pale

Through the red heat of noon;
In the twilight of dawn
Fairies broke fast with us;
Prophets led us on,
Heroes were kind to us
Day after happy day;
Many white Madonnas
We met on our way —
Farmer and longshoreman,
Fisherman and wife,
Children and laborers
Brave enough for Life,
Simple folk that Christ loved —
They were our friends. . . .

Dear, we must go again
To where the town ends. . .
Marguerite Wilkinson

IN THE MUSHROOM MEADOWS

SUN on the dewy grasslands where late the frost hath
shone,
And lo, what elfin cities are these we come upon!
What pigmy domes and thatches, what Arab caravan,
What downy-roofed pagodas that have known no
touch of man!
Are these the oldtime meadows? Yes, the wildgrape
scents the air;
The breath of ripened orchards still is incense every-
where;
Yet do these dawn-encampments bring the lurking
memories
Of Egypt and of Burma and the shores of China Seas.
Thomas Walsh

THE PATH THAT LEADS TO NOWHERE

THERE's a path that leads to Nowhere
  In a meadow that I know,
Where an inland island rises
  And the stream is still and slow;
There it wanders under willows
  And beneath the silver green
Of the birches' silent shadows
  Where the early violets lean.

Other pathways lead to Somewhere,
  But the one I love so well
Had no end and no beginning —
  Just the beauty of the dell,
Just the windflowers and the lilies
  Yellow striped as adder's tongue,
Seem to satisfy my pathway
  As it winds their sweets among.

There I go to meet the Springtime,
  When the meadow is aglow,
Marigolds amid the marshes, —
  And the stream is still and slow. —
There I find my fair oasis,
  And with care-free feet I tread
For the pathway leads to Nowhere,
  And the blue is overhead!

All the ways that lead to Somewhere
  Echo with the hurrying feet
Of the Struggling and the Striving,
  But the way I find so sweet

Bids me dream and bids me linger,
  Joy and Beauty are its goal, —
On the path that leads to Nowhere
  I have sometimes found my soul!
        Corinne Roosevelt Robinson

DAYS

SOME days my thoughts are just cocoons — all cold,
    and dull, and blind,
They hang from dripping branches in the grey woods
    of my mind;

And other days they drift and shine — such free and
    flying things!
I find the gold-dust in my hair, left by their brushing
    wings.
        Karle Wilson Baker

ELLIS PARK

LITTLE park that I pass through,
I carry off a piece of you
Every morning hurrying down
To my work-day in the town;
Carry you for country there
To make the city ways more fair.
I take your trees,
And your breeze,
Your greenness,
Your cleanness,
Some of your shade, some of your sky,
Some of your calm as I go by;

A NOTE FROM THE PIPES

Your flowers to trim
The pavements grim; *inversion* !
Your space for room in the jostled street
And grass for carpet to my feet.
Your fountains take and sweet bird calls
To sing me from my office walls.
All that I can see
I carry off with me.
But you never miss my theft,
So much treasure you have left.
As I find you, fresh at morning,
So I find you, home returning —
Nothing lacking from your grace.
All your riches wait in place
For me to borrow
On the morrow.

Do you hear this praise of you,
Little park that I pass through?

Helen Hoyt

A NOTE FROM THE PIPES

PAN, blow your pipes and I will be
Your fern, your pool, your dream, your tree!

I heard you play, caught your swift eye,
"A pretty melody!" called I,
"Hail, Pan!" And sought to pass you by.

Now blow your pipes and I will sing
To your sure lips' accompanying!

Wild God, who lifted me from earth,
Who taught me freedom, wisdom, mirth,
Immortalized my body's worth, —

Blow, blow your pipes! And from afar
I 'll come — I 'll be your bird, your star,
Your wood, your nymph, your kiss, your rhyme,
And all your godlike summer-time!

Leonora Speyer

AFTERNOON ON A HILL

I WILL be the gladdest thing
    Under the sun!
I will touch a hundred flowers
    And not pick one.

I will look at cliffs and clouds
    With quiet eyes,
Watch the wind bow down the grass,
    And the grass rise.

And when lights begin to show
    Up from the town,
I will mark which must be mine,
    And then start down!

Edna St. Vincent Millay

OPEN WINDOWS

OUT of the window a sea of green trees
    Lift their soft boughs like the arms of a dancer;
They beckon and call me, "Come out in the sun!"
    But I cannot answer.

I am alone with Weakness and Pain,
  Sick abed and June is going,
I cannot keep her, she hurries by
  With the silver-green of her garments blowing.

Men and women pass in the street
  Glad of the shining sapphire weather;
But we know more of it than they,
  Pain and I together.

They are the runners in the sun,
  Breathless and blinded by the race,
But we are watchers in the shade
  Who speak with Wonder face to face.
                              Sara Teasdale

OLD AMAZE

MINE eyes are filled today with old amaze
  At mountains, and at meadows deftly strewn
  With bits of the gay jewelry of June
And of her splendid vesture; and, agaze,
I stand where Spring her bright brocade of days
  Embroidered o'er, and listen to the flow
  Of sudden runlets — the faint blasts they blow.
Low, on their stony bugles, in still ways.
For wonders are at one, confederate yet:
  Yea, where the wearied year came to a close,
  An odor reminiscent of the rose;
And everywhere her seal has Summer set;
  And, as of old, in the horizon-sky,
  The sun can find a lovely place to die.
                              Mahlon Leonard Fisher

VOYAGE À L'INFINI

THE swan existing
Is like a song with an accompaniment
Imaginary.

Across the grassy lake,
Across the lake to the shadow of the willows,
It is accompanied by an image,
— as by Debussy's
"Reflets dans l'eau."

The swan that is
Reflects
Upon the solitary water — breast to breast
With the duplicity:
"*The other one!*"

And breast to breast it is confused.
O visionary wedding! O stateliness of the procession!
It is accompanied by the image of itself
Alone.

At night
The lake is a wide silence,
Without imagination.

Walter Conrad Arensberg

AFTER SUNSET

I HAVE an understanding with the hills
At evening when the slanted radiance fills
Their hollows, and the great winds let them be,
And they are quiet and look down at me.

Oh, then I see the patience in their eyes
Out of the centuries that made them wise.
They lend me hoarded memory and I learn
Their thoughts of granite and their whims of fern,
And why a dream of forests must endure
Though every tree be slain: and how the pure,
Invisible beauty has a word so brief
A flower can say it or a shaken leaf,
But few may ever snare it in a song,
Though for the quest a life is not too long.
When the blue hills grow tender, when they pull
The twilight close with gesture beautiful,
And shadows are their garments, and the air
Deepens, and the wild veery is at prayer, —
Their arms are strong around me; and I know
That somehow I shall follow when you go
To the still land beyond the evening star,
Where everlasting hills and valleys are:
And silence may not hurt us any more,
And terror shall be past, and grief, and war.

Grace Hazard Conkling

MORNING SONG OF SENLIN

It is morning, Senlin says, and in the morning
When the light drips through the shutters like the
    dew,
I arise, I face the sunrise,
And do the things my fathers learned to do.
Stars in the purple dusk above the rooftops
Pale in a saffron mist and seem to die,
And I myself on a swiftly tilting planet
Stand before a glass and tie my tie.

Vine leaves tap my window,
Dew-drops sing to the garden stones,
The robin chirps in the chinaberry tree
Repeating three clear tones.

It is morning. I stand by the mirror
And tie my tie once more.
While waves far off in a pale rose twilight
Crash on a white sand shore.
I stand by a mirror and comb my hair:
How small and white my face! —
The green earth tilts through a sphere of air
And bathes in a flame of space.
There are houses hanging above the stars
And stars hung under a sea . . .
And a sun far off in a shell of silence
Dapples my walls for me . . .

It is morning, Senlin says, and in the morning
Should I not pause in the light to remember God?
Upright and firm I stand on a star unstable,
He is immense and lonely as a cloud.
I will dedicate this moment before my mirror
To him alone, for him I will comb my hair.
Accept these humble offerings, cloud of silence!
I will think of you as I descend the stair.

Vine leaves tap my window,
The snail-track shines on the stones,
Dew-drops flash from the chinaberry tree
Repeating two clear tones.

It is morning, I awake from a bed of silence,
Shining I rise from the starless waters of sleep.

The walls are about me still as in the evening,
I am the same, and the same name still I keep.
The earth revolves with me, yet makes no motion,
The stars pale silently in a coral sky.
In a whistling void I stand before my mirror,
Unconcerned, and tie my tie.

There are horses neighing on far-off hills
Tossing their long white manes,
And mountains flash in the rose-white dusk,
Their shoulders black with rains . . .
It is morning. I stand by the mirror
And surprise my soul once more;
The blue air rushes above my ceiling,
There are suns beneath my floor . . .

. . . It is morning, Senlin says, I ascend from dark-
ness
And depart on the winds of space for I know not
where,
My watch is wound, a key is in my pocket,
And the sky is darkened as I descend the stair.
There are shadows across the windows, clouds in
heaven,
And a god among the stars; and I will go
Thinking of him as I might think of daybreak
And humming a tune I know . . .

Vine-leaves tap at the window,
Dew-drops sing to the garden stones,
The robin chirps in the chinaberry tree
Repeating three clear tones.

                                        Conrad Aiken

GOOD COMPANY

To-day I have grown taller from walking with the trees,
The seven sister-poplars who go softly in a line;
And I think my heart is whiter for its parley with a star
That trembled out at nightfall and hung above the pine.

The call-note of a redbird from the cedars in the dusk
Woke his happy mate within me to an answer free
    and fine;
And a sudden angel beckoned from a column of blue
    smoke —
Lord, who am I that they should stoop — these holy folk
    of thine?

                          Karle Wilson Baker

"FEUERZAUBER"

I never knew the earth had so much gold —
    The fields run over with it, and this hill,
Hoary and old,
    Is young with buoyant blooms that flame and thrill.

Such golden fires, such yellow — lo, how good
    This spendthrift world, and what a lavish God —
This fringe of wood,
    Blazing with buttercup and goldenrod.

You too, beloved, are changed. Again I see
    Your face grow mystical, as on that night
You turned to me,
    And all the trembling world — and you — were
    white.

Aye, you are touched; your singing lips grow dumb;
  The fields absorb you, color you entire . . .
And you become
  A goddess standing in a world of fire!

Louis Untermeyer

BIRCHES

WHEN I see birches bend to left and right
Across the lines of straighter darker trees,
I like to think some boy's been swinging them.
But swinging does n't bend them down to stay.
Ice-storms do that. Often you must have seen them
Loaded with ice a sunny winter morning
After a rain. They click upon themselves
As the breeze rises, and turn many-colored
As the stir cracks and crazes their enamel.
Soon the sun's warmth makes them shed crystal shells,
Shattering and avalanching on the snow-crust —
Such heaps of broken glass to sweep away
You 'd think the inner dome of heaven had fallen.
They are dragged to the withered bracken by the load,
And they seem not to break; though once they are
        bowed
So low for long, they never right themselves:
You may see their trunks arching in the woods
Years afterwards, trailing their leaves on the ground
Like girls on hands and knees that throw their hair
Before them over their heads to dry in the sun.
But I was going to say when Truth broke in
With all her matter-of-fact about the ice-storm
(Now am I free to be poetical?)
I should prefer to have some boy bend them

As he went out and in to fetch the cows —
Some boy too far from town to learn baseball,
Whose only play was what he found himself,
Summer or winter, and could play alone.
One by one he subdued his father's trees
By riding them down over and over again
Until he took the stiffness out of them,
And not one but hung limp, not one was left
For him to conquer. He learned all there was
To learn about not launching out too soon
And so not carrying the tree away
Clear to the ground. He always kept his poise
To the top branches, climbing carefully
With the same pains you use to fill a cup
Up to the brim, and even above the brim.
Then he flung outward, feet first, with a swish,
Kicking his way down through the air to the ground.
So was I once myself a swinger of birches.
And so I dream of going back to be.
It's when I'm weary of considerations,
And life is too much like a pathless wood
Where your face burns and tickles with the cobwebs
Broken across it, and one eye is weeping
From a twig's having lashed across it open.
I'd like to get away from earth awhile
And then come back to it and begin over.
May no fate willfully misunderstand me
And half grant what I wish and snatch me away
Not to return. Earth's the right place for love:
I don't know where it's likely to go better.
I'd like to go by climbing a birch tree,
And climb black branches up a snow-white trunk
Toward heaven, till the tree could bear no more,

But dipped its top and set me down again.
That would be good both going and coming back.
One could do worse than be a swinger of birches.

Robert Frost

FIFTY YEARS SPENT

Fifty years spent before I found me,
Wind on my mouth and the'taste of the rain,
Where the great hills circled and swept around me
And the torrents leapt to the mist-drenched plain;
Ah, it was long this coming of me
Back to the hills and the sounding sea.

Ye who can go when so it tideth
To fallow fields when the Spring is new,
Finding the spirit that there abideth,
Taking fill of the sun and the dew;
Little ye know of the cross of the town
And the small pale folk who go up and down.

Fifty years spent before I found me
A bank knee-deep with climbing rose,
Saw, or had space to look around me,
Knew how the apple buds and blows;
And all the while that I thought me wise
I walked as one with blinded eyes.

Scarcely a lad who passes twenty
But finds him a girl to balm his heart;
Only I, who had work so plenty,
Bade this loving keep apart:
Once I saw a girl in a crowd,
But I hushed my heart when it cried out aloud.

City courts in January, —
City courts in wilted June,
Often ye will catch and carry
Echoes of some straying tune:
Ah, but underneath the feet
Echo stifles in a street.

Fifty years spent, and what do they bring me?
Now I can buy the meadow and hill:
Where is the heart of the boy to sing thee?
Where is the life for thy living to fill?
And thirty years back in a city crowd
I passed a girl when my heart cried loud!

Maxwell Struthers Burt

THE CITY

WHEN, sick of all the sorrow and distress
    That flourished in the City like foul weeds,
    I sought blue rivers and green, opulent meads,
And leagues of unregarded loneliness
Whereon no foot of man had seemed to press,
    I did not know how great had been my needs,
    How wise the woodland's gospels and her creeds,
How good her faith to one long comfortless.

But in the silence came a Voice to me;
    In every wind it murmured, and I knew
    It would not cease though far my heart might roam.
It called me in the sunrise and the dew,
    At noon and twilight, sadly, hungrily,
    The jealous City, whispering always — "Home!"

Charles Hanson Towne

THE MOST-SACRED MOUNTAIN

Space, and the twelve clean winds of heaven,
And this sharp exultation, like a cry, after the slow
    six thousand steps of climbing!
This is Tai Shan, the beautiful, the most holy.

Below my feet the foot-hills nestle, brown with flecks
    of green; and lower down the flat brown plain,
    the floor of earth, stretches away to blue in-
    finity.
Beside me in this airy space the temple roofs cut their
    slow curves against the sky,   •
And one black bird circles above the void.

Space, and the twelve clean winds are here;
And with them broods eternity — a swift, white peace,
    a presence manifest.
The rhythm ceases here. Time has no place. This is
    the end that has no end.

Here, when Confucius came, a half a thousand years
    before the Nazarene, he stepped, with me, thus
    into timelessness.
The stone beside us waxes old, the carven stone that
    says: "On this spot once Confucius stood and
    felt the smallness of the world below."
The stone grows old:
Eternity is not for stones.
But I shall go down from this airy place, this swift
    white peace, this stinging exultation.

And time will close about me, and my soul stir to the
     rhythm of the daily round.
Yet, having known, life will not press so close,
       and always I shall feel time ravel thin about me;
For once I stood
In the white windy presence of eternity.

                   Eunice Tietjens

THE CHANT OF THE COLORADO

(*At the Grand Canyon*)

My brother, man, shapes him a plan
    And builds him a house in a day,
But I have toiled through a million years
    For a home to last alway.
I have flooded the sands and washed them
       down,
    I have cut through gneiss and granite.
No toiler of earth has wrought as I,
    Since God's first breath began it.
High mountain-buttes I have chiselled, to
       shade
    My wanderings to the sea.
With the wind's aid, and the cloud's aid,
Unweary and mighty and unafraid,
    I have bodied eternity.

My brother, man, builds for a span:
    His life is a moment's breath.
But I have hewn for a million years,
    Nor a moment dreamt of death.
By moons and stars I have measured my task —
    And some from the skies have perished:

But ever I cut and flashed and foamed,
    As ever my aim I cherished:
My aim to quarry the heart of earth,
    Till, in the rock's red rise,
Its age and birth, through an awful girth
Of strata, should show the wonder-worth
    Of patience to all eyes.

My brother, man, builds as he can,
    And beauty he adds for his joy,
But all the hues of sublimity
    My pinnacled walls employ.
Slow shadows iris them all day long,
    And silvery veils, soul-stilling,
The moon drops down their precipices,
    Soft with a spectral thrilling.
For all immutable dreams that sway
    With beauty the earth and air,
Are ever at play, by night and day,
My house of eternity to array
    In visions ever fair.

Cale Young Rice

THE WATER OUZEL

LITTLE brown surf-bather of the mountains!
Spirit of foam, lover of cataracts, shaking your wings
    in falling waters!
Have you no fear of the roar and rush when Nevada
    plunges —
Nevada, the shapely dancer, feeling her way with slim
    white fingers?

How dare you dash at Yosemite the mighty —
Tall, white limbed Yosemite, leaping down, down over
    the cliff?
Is it not enough to lean on the blue air of moun-
    tains?
Is it not enough to rest with your mate at timberline,
    in bushes that hug the rocks?
Must you fly through mad waters where the heaped-up
    granite breaks them?
Must you batter your wings in the torrent?
Must you plunge for life and death through the foam?

Harriet Monroe

OLD MANUSCRIPT

THE sky
Is that beautiful old parchment
In which the sun
And the moon
Keep their diary.
To read it all,
One must be a linguist
More learned than Father Wisdom;
And a visionary
More clairvoyant than Mother Dream.
But to feel it,
One must be an apostle:
One who is more than intimate
In having been, always,
The only confidant —
Like the earth
Or the sky.

Alfred Kreymborg

THE RUNNER IN THE SKIES

WHO is the runner in the skies,
With her blowing scarf of stars,
And our Earth and sun hovering like bees about her
      blossoming heart?
Her feet are on the winds, where space is deep,
Her eyes are nebulous and veiled,
She hurries through the night to a far lover.

James Oppenheim

EVENING SONG OF SENLIN

IT is moonlight. Alone in the silence
I ascend my stairs once more,
While waves, remote in a pale blue starlight,
Crash on a white sand shore.
It is moonlight. The garden is silent.
I stand in my room alone.
Across my wall, from the far-off moon,
A rain of fire is thrown . . .

There are houses hanging above the stars,
And stars hung under a sea:
And a wind from the long blue vault of time
Waves my curtains for me . . .

I wait in the dark once more,
Swung between space and space:
Before my mirror I lift my hands
And face my remembered face.
Is it I who stand in a question here,
Asking to know my name? . . .

It is I, yet I know not whither I go,
Nor why, nor whence I came.

It is I, who awoke at dawn
And arose and descended the stair,
Conceiving a god in the eye of the sun, —
In a woman's hands and hair.
It is I whose flesh is grey with the stones
I builded into a wall:
With a mournful melody in my brain
Of a tune I cannot recall . . .

There are roses to kiss: and mouths to kiss;
And the sharp-pained shadow of death.
I remember a rain-drop on my cheek, —
A wind like a fragrant breath . . .
And the star I laugh on tilts through heaven;
And the heavens are dark and steep . . .
I will forget these things once more
In the silence of sleep.

                                    Conrad Aiken

A THRUSH IN THE MOONLIGHT

In came the moon and covered me with wonder,
Touched me and was near me and made me very still
In came a rush of song, like rain after thunder,
Pouring importunate on my window-sill.

I lowered my head, I hid it, I would not see nor hear,
The birdsong had stricken me, had brought the moon
        too near.

But when I dared to lift my head, night began to
    fill
With singing in the darkness. And then the thrush
    grew still.
  And the moon came in, and silence, on my window-
    sill.

Witter Bynner

ORCHARD

I saw the first pear
As it fell —
The honey-seeking, golden-banded,
The yellow swarm
Was not more fleet than I,
(Spare us from loveliness)
And I fell prostrate
Crying:
You have flayed us
With your blossoms,
Spare us the beauty
Of fruit-trees.

The honey-seeking
Paused not,
The air thundered their song,
And I alone was prostrate.

O rough-hewn
God of the orchard,
I bring you an offering —
Do you, alone unbeautiful,

Son of the god,
Spare us from loveliness:

These fallen hazel-nuts,
Stripped late of their green sheaths,
Grapes, red-purple,
Their berries
Dripping with wine,
Pomegranates already broken,
And shrunken figs
And quinces untouched,
I bring you as offering.

H. D.

HEAT

O wind, rend open the heat,
Cut apart the heat,
Rend it to tatters.

Fruit cannot drop
Through this thick air —
Fruit cannot fall into heat
That presses up and blunts
The points of pears
And rounds the grapes.

Cut the heat —
Plough through it,
Turning it on either side
Of your path.

H. D.

MADONNA OF THE EVENING FLOWERS [1]

ALL day long I have been working,
Now I am tired.
I call: "Where are you?"
But there is only the oak tree rustling in the wind.
The house is very quiet,
The sun shines in on your books,
On your scissors and thimble just put down,
But you are not there.
Suddenly I am lonely:
Where are you?
I go about searching.

Then I see you,
Standing under a spire of pale blue larkspur,
With a basket of roses on your arm.
You are cool, like silver,
And you smile.
I think the Canterbury bells are playing little tunes.

You tell me that the peonies need spraying,
That the columbines have overrun all bounds,
That the pyrus japonica should be cut back and
    rounded.
You tell me these things.
But I look at you, heart of silver,
White heart-flame of polished silver,
Burning beneath the blue steeples of the larkspur.
And I long to kneel instantly at your feet,
While all about us peal the loud, sweet *Te Deums* of the
    Canterbury bells.

Amy Lowell

[1] Reprinted, by permission of the publishers, from *Pictures of the Flood
ing World,* by Amy Lowell. Copyright, 1919, by The Macmillan Company

THE NEW GOD

YE morning-glories, ring in the gale your bells,
And with dew water the walk's dust for the burden-
      bearing ants:
Ye swinging spears of the larkspur, open your wells of
      gold
And pay your honey-tax to the hummingbird . . .

O now I see by the opening of blossoms,
And of bills of the hungry fledglings,
And the bright travel of sun-drunk insects,
Morning's business is afoot: Earth is busied with a
      million mouths!

Where goes eaten grass and thrush-snapped dragon-
      fly?
Creation eats itself, to spawn in swarming sun-rays . . .
Bull and cricket go to it: life lives on life . . .
But O, ye flame-daubed irises, and ye hosts of gnats,
Like a well of light moving in morning's light,
What is this garmented animal that comes eating and
      drinking among you?
What is this upright one, with spade and with shears?

He is the visible and the invisible,
Behind his mouth and his eyes are other mouth and
      eyes . . .
Thirster after visions
He sees the flowers to their roots and the Earth back
      through its silent ages:
He parts the sky with his gaze:

He flings a magic on the hills, clothing them with
    Upanishad music,
Peopling the valley with dreamed images that van-
    ished in Greece millenniums back;
And in the actual morning, out of longing, shapes on
    the hills
To-morrow's golden grandeur . . .

O ye million hungerers and ye sun-rays
Ye are the many mothers of this invisible god,
This Earth's star and sun that rises singing and toiling
    among you,
This that is I, in joy, in the garden,
Singing to you, ye morning-glories,
Calling to you, ye swinging spears of the larkspur.
                     James Oppenheim

PATTERNS [1]

I WALK down the garden paths,
And all the daffodils
Are blowing, and the bright blue squills.
I walk down the patterned garden-paths
In my stiff, brocaded gown.
With my powdered hair and jewelled fan,
I too am a rare
Pattern. As I wander down
The garden paths.

My dress is richly figured,
And the train

[1] Reprinted, by permission of the publishers, from *Men, Women and Ghosts*, by Amy Lowell.   Copyright, 1916, by The Macmillan Company.

Makes a pink and silver stain
On the gravel, and the thrift
Of the borders.
Just a plate of current fashion,
Tripping by in high-heeled, ribboned shoes.
Not a softness anywhere about me,
Only whalebone and brocade.
And I sink on a seat in the shade
Of a lime tree. For my passion
Wars against the stiff brocade.
The daffodils and squills
Flutter in the breeze
As they please.
And I weep;
For the lime tree is in blossom
And one small flower has dropped upon my bosom.

And the plashing of waterdrops
In the marble fountain
Comes down the garden-paths.
The dripping never stops.
Underneath my stiffened gown
Is the softness of a woman bathing in a marble basin,
A basin in the midst of hedges grown
So thick, she cannot see her lover hiding,
But she guesses he is near,
And the sliding of the water
Seems the stroking of a dear
Hand upon her.
What is Summer in a fine brocaded gown!
I should like to see it lying in a heap upon the
      ground.
All the pink and silver crumpled up on the ground.

I would be the pink and silver as I ran along the
    paths,
And he would stumble after,
Bewildered by my laughter.
I should see the sun flashing from his sword-hilt and
    the buckles on his shoes.
I would choose
To lead him in a maze along the patterned paths,
A bright and laughing maze for my heavy-booted lover.
Till he caught me in the shade,
And the buttons of his waistcoat bruised my body as
    he clasped me,
Aching, melting, unafraid.
With the shadows of the leaves and the sundrops,
And the plopping of the waterdrops,
All about us in the open afternoon —
I am very like to swoon
With the weight of this brocade,
For the sun sifts through the shade.

Underneath the fallen blossom
In my bosom,
Is a letter I have hid.
It was brought to me this morning by a rider from
    the Duke.
"Madam, we regret to inform you that Lord Hartwell
Died in action Thursday se'nnight."
As I read it in the white, morning sunlight,
The letters squirmed like snakes.
"Any answer, Madam," said my footman.
"No," I told him.
"See that the messenger takes some refreshment.
No, no answer."

And I walked into the garden,
Up and down the patterned paths,
In my stiff, correct brocade.
The blue and yellow flowers stood up proudly in the
      sun,
Each one.
I stood upright too,
Held rigid to the pattern
By the stiffness of my gown.
Up and down I walked,
Up and down.

In a month he would have been my husband.
In a month, here, underneath this lime,
We would have broke the pattern;
He for me, and I for him,
He as Colonel, I as Lady,
On this shady seat.
He had a whim
That sunlight carried blessing.
And I answered, "It shall be as you have said."
Now he is dead.

In Summer and in Winter I shall walk
Up and down
The patterned garden-paths
In my stiff, brocaded gown.
The squills and daffodils
Will give place to pillared roses, and to asters, and
      to snow.
I shall go
Up and down
In my gown.

Gorgeously arrayed,
Boned and stayed.
And the softness of my body will be guarded from
      embrace
By each button, hook, and lace.
For the man who should loose me is dead,
Fighting with the Duke in Flanders,
In a pattern called a war.
Christ! What are patterns for?

Amy Lowell

RICHARD CORY

WHENEVER Richard Cory went down town,
We people on the pavement looked at him:
He was a gentleman from sole to crown,
Clean favored, and imperially slim.

And he was always quietly arrayed,
And he was always human when he talked;
But still he fluttered pulses when he said,
"Good-morning," and he glittered when he walked.

And he was rich, — yes, richer than a king, —
And admirably schooled in every grace:
In fine, we thought that he was everything
To make us wish that we were in his place.

So on we worked, and waited for the light,
And went without the meat, and cursed the bread;
And Richard Cory, one calm summer night,
Went home and put a bullet through his head.

Edwin Arlington Robinson

OF ONE SELF-SLAIN

WHEN he went blundering back to God,
  His songs half written, his work half done,
Who knows what paths his bruised feet trod,
  What hills of peace or pain he won?

I hope God smiled and took his hand,
  And said, "Poor truant, passionate fool!
Life's book is hard to understand:
  Why couldst thou not remain at school?"
                  Charles Hanson Towne

THE SILENT FOLK

OH, praise me not the silent folk;
To me they only seem
Like leafless, bird-abandoned oak
And muffled, frozen stream.

I want the leaves to talk and tell
The joy that's in the tree,
And water-nymphs to weave a spell
Of pixie melody.

Your silent folk may be sincere,
But still, when all is said,
We have to grant they're rather drear, —
And maybe, too, they're dead.
                  Charles Wharton Stork

CONVENTION

THE snow is lying very deep.
My house is sheltered from the blast.
I hear each muffled step outside,
I hear each voice go past.

But I'll not venture in the drift
Out of this bright security,
Till enough footsteps come and go
To make a path for me.

Agnes Lee

MAD BLAKE

BLAKE saw a treeful of angels at Peckham Rye,
And his hands could lay hold on the tiger's terrible
      heart.
Blake knew how deep is Hell, and Heaven how high,
And could build the universe from one tiny part.
Blake heard the asides of God, as with furrowed brow
He sifts the star-streams between the Then and the
      Now,
In vast infant sagacity brooding, an infant's grace
Shining serene on his simple, benignant face.

Blake was mad, they say, — and Space's Pandora-box
Loosed its wonders upon him — devils, but angels
      indeed.
I, they say, am sane, but no key of mine unlocks
One lock of one gate wherethrough Heaven's glory is
      freed.

And I stand and I hold my breath, daylong, yearlong,
Out of comfort and easy dreaming evermore starting
    awake, —
Yearning beyond all sanity for some echo of that Song
Of Songs that was sung to the soul of the madman,
    Blake!

Wm. Rose Benét

THE NAME

WHEN I come back from secret dreams
    In gardens deep and fair,
How very curious it seems —
    This mortal name I bear.

For by this name I make their bread
    And trim the household light
And sun the linen for the bed
    And close the door at night.

I wonder who myself may be,
    And whence it was I came —
Before the Church had laid on me
    This frail and earthly name.

My sponsors spake unto the Lord
    And three things promised they,
Upon my soul with one accord
    Their easy vows did lay.

My ancient spirit heard them not.
    I think it was not there.
But in a place they had forgot
    It drank a starrier air.

Yes, in a silent place and deep —
   There did it dance and run,
And sometimes it lay down to sleep
   Or sprang into the sun.

The Priest saw not my aureole shine!
   My sweet wings saw not he!
He graved me with a solemn sign
   And laid a name on me.

Now by this name I stitch and mend,
   The daughter of my home,
By this name do I save and spend
   And when they call, I come.

But oh, that Name, that other Name,
   More secret and more mine!
It burns as does the angelic flame
   Before the midmost shrine.

Before my soul to earth was brought
   Into God's heart it came,
He wrote a meaning in my thought
   And gave to me a Name.

By this Name do I ride the air
   And dance from star to star,
And I behold all things are fair,
   For I see them as they are.

I plunge into the deepest seas,
   In flames I, laughing, burn.
In roseate clouds I take my ease
   Nor to the earth return.

It is my beauteous Name — my own —
　　That I have never heard.
God keeps it for Himself alone,
　　That strange and lovely word.

God keeps it for Himself — but yet
　　You are His voice, and so
In your heart He is calling me,
　　And unto you I go.

Love, by this Name I sing, and breathe
　　A fresh, mysterious air.
By this I innocently wreathe
　　New garlands for my hair.

By this Name I am born anew
　　More beautiful, more bright.
More roseate than angelic dew,
　　Apparelled in delight.

I'll sing and stitch and make the bread
　　In the wonder of my Name,
And sun the linen for the bed
　　And tend the fireside flame.

By this Name do I answer yes —
　　Word beautiful and true.
By this I'll sew the bridal dress
　　I shall put on for you.
　　　　　　　　Anna Hempstead Branch

SONGS OF AN EMPTY HOUSE

VISTA

BEFORE I die I may be great,
    The chanting guest of kings,
A queen in wonderlands of song
    Where every blossom sings.
I may put on a golden gown
    And walk in sunny light,
Carrying in my hair the day,
    And in my eyes the night.

It may be men will honor me —
    The wistful ones and wise,
Who know the ruth of victory,
    The joy of sacrifice.
I may be rich, I may be gay,
    But all the crowns grow old —
The laurel withers and the bay
    And dully rusts the gold.

Before I die I may break bread
    With many queens and kings —
Oh, take the golden gown away,
    For there are other things —
And I shall miss the love of babes
    With flesh of rose and pearl,
The dewy eyes, the budded lips —
    A boy, a little girl.

THE END

My father got me strong and straight and slim,
    And I give thanks to him;

My mother bore me glad and sound and sweet, -
 I kiss her feet.

But now, with me, their generation fails,
 And nevermore avails
To cast through me the ancient mould again,
 Such women and men.

I have no son, whose life of flesh and fire
 Sprang from my splendid sire,
No daughter for whose soul my mother's flesh
 Wrought raiment fresh.

Life's venerable rhythms like a flood
 Beat in my brain and blood,
Crying from all the generations past,
 "Is this the last?"

And I make answer to my haughty dead,
 Who made me, heart and head,
"Even the sunbeams falter, flicker and bend —
 I am the end."
      · *Marguerite Wilkinson*

THE HILL WIFE

LONELINESS

(Her Word)

ONE ought not to have to care
 So much as you and I
Care when the birds come round the house
 To seem to say good-bye;

Or care so much when they come back
    With whatever it is they sing;
The truth being we are as much
    Too glad for the one thing

As we are too sad for the other here —
    With birds that fill their breasts
But with each other and themselves
    And their built or driven nests.

HOUSE FEAR

ALWAYS — I tell you this they learned —
Always at night when they returned
To the lonely house from far away,
To lamps unlighted and fire gone gray,
They learned to rattle the lock and key
To give whatever might chance to be
Warning and time to be off in flight:
And preferring the out- to the in-door night,
They learned to leave the house-door wide
Until they had lit the lamp inside.

THE OFT-REPEATED DREAM

SHE had no saying dark enough
    For the dark pine that kept
Forever trying the window-latch
    Of the room where they slept.

The tireless but ineffectual hands
    That with every futile pass
Made the great tree seem as a little bird
    Before the mystery of glass!

It never had been inside the room,
   And only one of the two
Was afraid in an oft-repeated dream
   Of what the tree might do.

THE IMPULSE

It was too lonely for her there,
   And too wild,
And since there were but two of them,
   And no child,

And work was little in the house,
   She was free,
And followed where he furrowed field,
   Or felled tree.

She rested on a log and tossed
   The fresh chips,
With a song only to herself
   On her lips.

And once she went to break a bough
   Of black alder.
She strayed so far she scarcely heard
   When he called her —

And did n't answer — did n't speak —
   Or return.
She stood, and then she ran and hid
   In the fern.

He never found her, though he looked
   Everywhere,

And he asked at her mother's house
    Was she there.

Sudden and swift and light as that
    The ties gave,
And he learned of finalities
    Besides the grave.

Robert Frost

A LOVE SONG

My love it should be silent, being deep —
And being very peaceful should be still —
Still as the utmost depths of ocean keep —
Serenely silent as some mighty hill.

Yet is my love so great it needs must fill
With very joy the inmost heart of me,
The joy of dancing branches on the hill
The joy of leaping waves upon the sea.

Theodosia Garrison

ENVOI

Belovèd, till the day break,
    Leave wide the little door;
And bless, to lack and longing,
    Our brimming more-and-more.

Is love a scanted portion,
    That we should hoard thereof? —
Oh, call unto the deserts,
    Belovèd and my Love!

Josephine Preston Peabody

OUR LITTLE HOUSE

OUR little house upon the hill
In winter time is strangely still;
The roof tree, bare of leaves, stands high,
A candelabrum for the sky,
And down below the lamplights glow,
And ours makes answer o'er the snow.

Our little house upon the hill
In summer time strange voices fill;
With ceaseless rustle of the leaves,
And birds that twitter in the eaves,
And all the vines entangled so
The village lights no longer show.

Our little house upon the hill
Is just the house of Jack and Jill,
And whether showing or unseen,
Hid behind its leafy screen;
There's a star that points it out
When the lamp lights are in doubt.

Thomas Walsh

THE HOMELAND

My land was the west land; my home was on the hill.
I never think of my land but it makes my heart to
thrill;
I never smell the west wind that blows the golden
skies,
But old desire is in my feet and dreams are in my
eyes.

My home crowned the high land; it had a stately
    grace.
I never think of my land but I see my mother's face;
I never smell the west wind that blows the silver ships
But old delight is in my heart and mirth is on my lips.

My land was a high land; my home was near the skies.
I never think of my land but a light is in my eyes;
I never smell the west wind that blows the summer
    rain —
But I am at my mother's knee, a little lad again.

                          Dana Burnet

CRADLE SONG

I

LORD GABRIEL, wilt thou not rejoice
When at last a little boy's
    Cheek lies heavy as a rose
    And his eyelids close?

Gabriel, when that hush may be,
This sweet hand all heedfully
    I'll undo for thee alone,
    From his mother's own.

Then the far blue highway paven
With the burning stars of heaven,
    He shall gladden with the sweet
    Hasting of his feet: —

Feet so brightly bare and cool,
Leaping, as from pool to pool;

From a little laughing boy
Splashing rainbow joy!

Gabriel, wilt thou understand
How to keep this hovering hand? —
      Never shut, as in a bond,
         From the bright beyond? —

Nay, but though it cling and close
Tightly as a climbing rose,
      Clasp it only so, — aright,
         Lest his heart take fright.

      (*Dormi, dormi, tu.*
      The dusk is hung with blue.)

II

Lord Michael, wilt not thou rejoice
When at last a little boy's
      Heart, a shut-in murmuring bee,
         Turns him unto thee?

Wilt thou heed thine armor well, —
To take his hand from Gabriel,
      So his radiant cup of dream
         May not spill a gleam?

He will take thy heart in thrall,
Telling o'er thy breastplate, all
      Colors, in his bubbling speech,
         With his hand to each.

      (*Dormi, dormi, tu.*
      Sapphire is the blue,

Pearl and beryl, they are called,
Crysoprase and emerald,
Sard and amethyst
Numbered so, and kissed.)

Ah, but find some angel-word
For thy sharp, subduing sword!
Yea, Lord Michael, make no doubt
He will find it out:

(Dormi, dormi, tu!
His eyes will look at you.)

III

Last, a little morning space,
Lead him to that leafy place
Where Our Lady sits awake,
For all mothers' sake.

Bosomed with the Blessèd One,
He shall mind her of her Son,
Once so folded from all harms
In her shrining arms.

(In her veil of blue,
Dormi, dormi, tu.)

So; — and fare thee well.
Softly, — Gabriel . . .
When the first faint red shall come,
Bid the Day-star lead him home,
For the bright world's sake,
To my heart, awake.
Josephine Preston Peabody

SLUMBER SONG

DROWSILY come the sheep
From the place where the pastures be,
        By a dusty lane
        To the fold again,
First one, and then two, and three:
    First one, then two, by the paths of sleep
    Drowsily come the sheep.

Drowsily come the sheep,
And the shepherd is singing low:
        After eight comes nine
        In the endless line,
They come, and then in they go.
    First eight, then nine, by the paths of sleep
    Drowsily come the sheep.

Drowsily come the sheep
And they pass through the sheepfold door;
        After one comes two,
        After one comes two,
Comes two and then three and four.
    First one, then two, by the paths of sleep,
    Drowsily come the sheep.

                              Louis V. Ledoux

BALLAD OF A CHILD [1]

YEARLY thrilled the plum tree
With the mother-mood;
Every June the rose stock

[1] Reprinted, by permission of the publishers, from *The Quest*, by John
G. Neihardt. Copyright, 1916, by The Macmillan Company.

Bore her wonder-child:
Every year the wheatlands
Reared a golden brood:
World of praying Rachaels,
Heard and reconciled!

"Poet," said the plum tree's
Singing white and green,
"What avails your mooning,
Can you fashion plums?"
"Dreamer," crooned the wheatland's
Rippling vocal sheen,
"See my golden children
Marching as with drums!"

"By a god begotten,"
Hymned the sunning vine,
"In my lyric children
Purple music flows!"
"Singer," breathed the rose bush,
"Are they not divine?"
"Have you any daughters
Mighty as a rose?"

Happy, happy mothers!
Cruel, cruel words!
Mine are ghostly children,
Haunting all the ways;
Latent in the plum bloom,
Calling through the birds,
Romping with the wheat brood
In their shadow plays!

Gotten out of star-glint,
Mothered of the Moon;
Nurtured with the rose scent,
Wild elusive throng!
Something of the vine's dream
Crept into a tune;
Something of the wheat-drone
Echoed in a song.

Once again the white fires
Smoked among the plums;
Once again the world-joy
Burst the crimson bud;
Golden-bannered wheat broods
Marched to fairy drums;
Once again the vineyard
Felt the Bacchic blood.

"Lo, he comes, — the dreamer" —
Crooned the whitened boughs,
"Quick with vernal love-fires —
Oh, at last he knows!
See the bursting plum bloom
There above his brows!"
"Boaster!" breathed the rose bush,
"'Tis a budding rose!"

Droned the glinting acres,
"In his soul, mayhap,
Something like a wheat-dream
Quickens into shape!"
Sang the sunning vineyard,
"Lo, the lyric sap

Sets his heart a-throbbing
Like a purple grape!"

Mother of the wheatlands,
Mother of the plums,
Mother of the vineyard —
All that loves and grows —
Such a living glory
To the dreamer comes,
Mystic as a wheat-song,
Mighty as a rose!

Star-glint, moon-glow,
Gathered in a mesh!
Spring-hope, white fire
By a kiss beguiled!
Something of the world-joy
Dreaming into flesh!
Bird-song, vine-thrill
Quickened to a child!

John G. Neihardt

AMBITION

KENTON and Deborah, Michael and Rose,
These are fine children as all the world knows,
But into my arms in my dreams every night
Come Peter and Christopher, Faith and Delight.

Kenton is tropical, Rose is pure white,
Deborah shines like a star in the night;
Michael's round eyes are as blue as the sea,
And nothing on earth could be dearer to me.

But where is the baby with Faith can compare?
What is the colour of Peterkin's hair?
Who can make Christopher clear to my sight,
Or show me the eyes of my daughter Delight?

When people inquire I always just state:
"I have four nice children and hope to have eight.
Though the first four are pretty and certain to please,
Who knows but the rest may be nicer than these?"
Aline Kilmer

THE GIFT

LET others give you wealth and love,
   And guard you while you live;
I cannot set my gift above
   The gifts that others give.

And yet the gift I give is good:
   In one man's eyes to see
The worship of your maidenhood
   While children climb your knee.
Louis V. Ledoux

THE ANCIENT BEAUTIFUL THINGS

I AM all alone in the room.
The evening stretches before me
Like a road all delicate gloom
Till it reaches the midnight's gate.
And I hear his step on the path,
And his questioning whistle, low
At the door as I hurry to meet him.

He will ask, "Are the doors all locked?
Is the fire made safe on the hearth?
And she — is she sound asleep?"

I shall say, "Yes, the doors are locked,
And the ashes are white as the frost:
Only a few red eyes
To stare at the empty room.
And she is all sound asleep,
Up there where the silence sings,
And the curtains stir in the cold."

He will ask, "And what did you do
While I have been gone so long?
So long! Four hours or five!"

I shall say, "There was nothing I did. —
I mended that sleeve of your coat.
And I made her a little white hood
Of the furry pieces I found
Up in the garret to-day.
She shall wear it to play in the snow,
Like a little white bear, — and shall laugh,
And tumble, and crystals of stars
Shall shine on her cheeks and hair.
— It was nothing I did. — I thought
You would never come home again!"

Then he will laugh out, low,
Being fond of my folly, perhaps;
And softly and hand in hand
We shall creep upstairs in the dusk
To look at her, lying asleep:
Our little gold bird in her nest:

The wonderful bird who flew in
At the window our Life flung wide.
(How should we have chosen her,
Had we seen them all in a row,
The unborn vague little souls,
All wings and tremulous hands?
How should we have chosen her,
Made like a star to shine,
Made like a bird to fly,
Out of a drop of our blood,
And earth, and fire, and God?)

Then we shall go to sleep,
Glad. —
          O God, did you know
When you moulded men out of clay,
Urging them up and up
Through the endless circles of change,
Travail and turmoil and death,
Many would curse you down,
Many would live all gray
With their faces flat like a mask:
But there would be some, O God,
Crying to you each night,
"I am so glad! so glad!
I am so rich and gay!
How shall I thank you, God?"

Was that one thing you knew
When you smiled and found it was good:
The curious teeming earth
That grew like a child at your hand?
Ah, you might smile, for that! —

— I am all alone in the room.
The books and the pictures peer,
Dumb old friends, from the dark.
The wind goes high on the hills,
And my fire leaps out, being proud.
The terrier, down on the hearth,
Twitches and barks in his sleep,
Soft little foolish barks,
More like a dream than a dog . . .

I will mend the sleeve of that coat,
All ragged, — and make her the hood
Furry, and white, for the snow.
She shall tumble and laugh . . .
                              Oh, I think
Though a thousand rivers of grief
Flood over my head, — though a hill
Of horror lie on my breast, —
Something will sing, "Be glad!
You have had all your heart's desire:
The unknown things that you asked
When you lay awake in the nights,
Alone, and searching the dark
For the secret wonder of life.
You have had them (can you forget?):
The ancient beautiful things!" . . .

How long he is gone. And yet
It is only an hour or two. . . .

Oh, I am so happy. My eyes
Are troubled with tears.
                    Did you know,

O God, they would be like this,
Your ancient beautiful things?
Are there more? Are there more, — out there? —
O God, are there always more?
                              Fannie Stearns Davis

MATER DOLOROSA [1]

O CLINGING hands, and eyes where sleep has set
  Her seal of peace, go not from me so soon.
O little feet, take not the pathway yet,
The dust of other feet with tears is wet,
And sorrow wanders there with slow regret;
  O eager feet, take not the path so soon.

Take it not yet, for death is at the end,
  And kingly death will wait until you come.
Full soon the feet of youth will turn the bend,
The eyes will see where followed footsteps wend.
Go not so soon, though death be found a friend;
  For kingly death will wait until you come.
                              Louis V. Ledoux

PREVISION

I KNOW you are too dear to stay;
  You are so exquisitely sweet:
My lonely house will thrill some day
  To echoes of your eager feet.

I hold your words within my heart,
  So few, so infinitely dear;
Watching your fluttering hands I start
  At the corroding touch of fear.

---

[1] Reprinted, by permission of the publishers, from *The Story of Eleusis,* by Louis V. Ledoux. Copyright, 1916, by The Macmillan Company.

A faint, unearthly music rings
   From you to Heaven — it is not far!
A mist about your beauty clings
   Like a thin cloud before a star.

My heart shall keep the child I knew,
   When you are really gone from me,
And spend its life remembering you
   As shells remember the lost sea.

               Aline Kilmer

"A WIND ROSE IN THE NIGHT"

A WIND rose in the night,
   (She had always feared it so!)
Sorrow plucked at my heart
   And I could not help but go.

Softly I went and stood
   By her door at the end of the hall.
Dazed with grief I watched
   The candles flaring and tall.

The wind was wailing aloud:
   I thought how she would have cried)
For my warm familiar arms
   And the sense of me by her side.

The candles flickered and leapt,
   The shadows jumped on the wall.
She lay before me small and still
   And did not care at all.

               Aline Kilmer

HOW MUCH OF GODHOOD

How much of Godhood did it take —
  What purging epochs had to pass,
Ere I was fit for leaf and lake
  And worthy of the patient grass?

What mighty travails must have been,
  What ages must have moulded me,
Ere I was raised and made akin
  To dawn, the daisy and the sea.

In what great struggles was I felled,
  In what old lives I labored long,
Ere I was given a world that held
  A meadow, butterflies and Song?

But oh, what cleansings and what fears,
  What countless raisings from the dead,
Ere I could see Her, touched with tears,
  Pillow the little weary head.
              Louis Untermeyer

THE FIRST FOOD

MOTHER, in some sad evening long ago,
  From thy young breast my groping lips were taken,
  Their hunger stilled, so soon again to waken,
But nevermore that holy food to know.

Ah! nevermore! for all the child might crave!
  Ah! nevermore! through years unkind and dreary!
  Often of other fare my lips are weary,
Unwearied once of what thy bosom gave.

(Poor wordless mouth that could not speak thy name!
  At what unhappy revels has it eaten
  The viands that no memory can sweeten, —
The banquet found eternally the same!)

Then fell a shadow first on thee and me,
  And tendrils broke that held us two how dearly!
  Once infinitely thine, then hourly, yearly,
Less thine, as less the worthy thine to be.

(O mouth that yet should kiss the mouth of Sin!
  Were lies so sweet, now bitter to remember?
  Slow sinks the flame unfaithful to an ember;
New beauty fades and passion's wine is thin.)

How poor an end of that solicitude
  And all the love I had not from another!
  Peace to thine unforgetting heart, O Mother,
Who gav'st the dear and unremembered food!

George Sterling

THE MONK IN THE KITCHEN

I

ORDER is a lovely thing;
On disarray it lays its wing,
Teaching simplicity to sing.
It has a meek and lowly grace,
Quiet as a nun's face.
Lo — I will have thee in this place!
Tranquil well of deep delight,
Transparent as the water, bright —

All things that shine through thee appear
As stones through water, sweetly clear.
Thou clarity,
That with angelic charity
Revealest beauty where thou art,
Spread thyself like a clean pool.
Then all the things that in thee are
Shall seem more spiritual and fair,
Reflections from serener air —
Sunken shapes of many a star
In the high heavens set afar.

II

Ye stolid, homely, visible things,
Above you all brood glorious wings
Of your deep entities, set high,
Like slow moons in a hidden sky.
But you, their likenesses, are spent
Upon another element.
Truly ye are but seemings —
The shadowy cast-off gleamings
Of bright solidities. Ye seem
Soft as water, vague as dream;
Image, cast in a shifting stream.

III

What are ye?
I know not.
Brazen pan and iron pot,
Yellow brick and grey flag-stone
That my feet have trod upon —
Ye seem to me
Vessels of bright mystery.

For ye do bear a shape, and so
Though ye were made by man, I know
An inner Spirit also made
And ye his breathings have obeyed.

IV

Shape the strong and awful Spirit,
Laid his ancient hand on you.
He waste chaos doth inherit;
He can alter and subdue.
Verily, he doth lift up
Matter, like a sacred cup.
Into deep substance he reached, and lo
Where ye were not, ye were; and so
Out of useless nothing, ye
Groaned and laughed and came to be.
And I use you, as I can,
Wonderful uses, made for man,
Iron pot and brazen pan.

V

What are ye?
I know not;
Nor what I really do
When I move and govern you.
There is no small work unto God.
He requires of us greatness;
Of his least creature
A high angelic nature,
Stature superb and bright completeness.
He sets to us no humble duty.
Each act that he would have us do
Is haloed round with strangest beauty.

Terrific deeds and cosmic tasks
Of his plainest child he asks.
When I polish the brazen pan
I hear a creature laugh afar
In the gardens of a star,
And from his burning presence run
Flaming wheels of many a sun.
Whoever makes a thing more bright,
He is an angel of all light.
When I cleanse this earthen floor
My spirit leaps to see
Bright garments trailing over it.
Wonderful lustres cover it,
A cleanness made by me.
Purger of all men's thoughts and ways,
With labor do I sound Thy praise,
My work is done for Thee.
Whoever makes a thing more bright,
He is an angel of all light.
Therefore let me spread abroad
The beautiful cleanness of my God.

VI

One time in the cool of dawn
Angels came and worked with me.
The air was soft with many a wing.
They laughed amid my solitude
And cast bright looks on everything.
Sweetly of me did they ask
That they might do my common task.
And all were beautiful — but one
With garments whiter than the sun

Had such a face
Of deep, remembered grace,
That when I saw I cried — "Thou art
The great Blood-Brother of my heart.
Where have I seen thee?" — And he said,
"When we are dancing 'round God's throne,
How often thou art there.
Beauties from thy hands have flown
Like white doves wheeling in mid-air.
Nay — thy soul remembers not?
Work on, and cleanse thy iron pot."

VII

What are we? I know not.
Anna Hempstead Branch

A SAINT'S HOURS

Her Matins

IN the still cold before the sun
    Her brothers and her sisters small
She woke, and washed and dressed each
    one.

Prime

And through the morning hours all
    Singing above her broom she stood
And swept the house from hall to hall.

Tierce

Then out she ran with tidings good
    Across the field and down the lane,
To share them with the neighborhood.

Sexts

Four miles she walked, and home again,
    To sit through half the afternoon
And hear a feeble crone complain.

Nones

But when she saw the frosty moon
And lakes of shadow on the hill,
Her maiden dreams grew bright as noon.

Vespers

She threw her pitying apron frill
Over a little trembling mouse
When the sleek cat yawned on the sill.

Evensong

In the late hours and drowsy house,
At last, too tired, beside her bed
She fell asleep — her prayers half said.

Sarah N. Cleghorn

A LADY [1]

You are beautiful and faded
Like an old opera tune
Played upon a harpsichord;
Or like the sun-flooded silks
Of an eighteenth-century boudoir.
In your eyes
Smoulder the fallen roses of out-lived minutes,
And the perfume of your soul
Is vague and suffusing,
With the pungence of sealed spice-jars.
Your half-tones delight me,
And I grow mad with gazing
At your blent colours.

[1] Reprinted, by permission of the publishers, from *Sword Blades and Poppy Seed*, by Amy Lowell. Copyright, 1914, by The Macmillan Company.

My vigour is a new-minted penny,
Which I cast at your feet.
Gather it up from the dust,
That its sparkle may amuse you.

Amy Lowell

THE CHILD IN ME

SHE follows me about my House of Life
(This happy little ghost of my dead Youth!)
She has no part in Time's relentless strife
She keeps her old simplicity and truth —
And laughs at grim Mortality,
This deathless Child that stays with me —
(This happy little ghost of my dead Youth!)

My House of Life is weather-stained with years —
(O Child in Me, I wonder why you stay.)
Its windows are bedimmed with rain of tears,
The walls have lost their rose, its thatch is gray.
One after one its guests depart,
So dull a host is my old heart.
(O Child in Me, I wonder why you stay!)

For jealous Age, whose face I would forget,
Pulls the bright flowers you bring me from my hair
And powders it with snow; and yet — and yet
I love your dancing feet and jocund air.
I have no taste for caps of lace
To tie about my faded face —
I love to wear your flowers in my hair.

O Child in Me, leave not my House of Clay
Until we pass together through the Door,
When lights are out, and Life has gone away
And we depart to come again no more.
We comrades who have travelled far
Will hail the Twilight and the Star,
And smiling, pass together through the Door!
May Riley Smith

THE SON

I HEARD an old farm-wife,
   Selling some barley,
Mingle her life with life
   And the name "Charley."

Saying, "The crop's all in,
   We're about through now;
Long nights will soon begin,
   We're just us two now.

Twelve bushels at sixty cents,
   It's all I carried —
He sickened making fence;
   He was to be married —

It feels like frost was near —
   His hair was curly.
The spring was late that year,
   But the harvest early."
Ridgely Torrence

MUY VIEJA MEXICANA

I'VE seen her pass with eyes upon the road —
An old bent woman in a bronze-black shawl,
With skin as dried and wrinkled as a mummy's,
As brown as a cigar-box, and her voice
Like the low vibrant strings of a guitar.
And I have fancied from the girls about
What she was at their age, what they will be
When they are old as she. But now she sits
And smokes away each night till dawn comes round,
Thinking, beside the piñons' flame, of days
Long past and gone, when she was young — content
To be no longer young, her epic done:

For a woman has work and much to do,
And it's good at the last to know it's through,
And still have time to sit alone,
To have some time you can call your own.
It's good at the last to know your mind
And travel the paths that you traveled blind,
To see each turn and even make
Trips in the byways you did not take —
But that, *por Dios*, is over and done,
It's pleasanter now in the way we've come;
It's good to smoke and none to say
What's to be done on the coming day,
No mouths to feed or coat to mend,
And none to call till the last long end.
Though one have sons and friends of one's own,
It's better at last to live alone.
For a man must think of food to buy,
And a woman's thoughts may be wild and high;

But when she is young she must curb her pride,
And her heart is tamed for the child at her side.
But when she is old her thoughts may go
Wherever they will, and none to know.
And night is the time to think and dream,
And not to get up with the dawn's first gleam;
Night is the time to laugh or weep,
And when dawn comes it is time to sleep . . .

When it's all over and there's none to care,
I mean to be like her and take my share
Of comfort when the long day's done,
And smoke away the nights, and see the sun
Far off, a shrivelled orange in a sky gone black,
Through eyes that open inward and look back.

Alice Corbin

HROLF'S THRALL, HIS SONG

THERE be five things to a man's desire:
Kine flesh, roof-tree, his own fire,
Clean cup of sweet wine from goat's hide,
And through dark night one to lie beside.

Four things poor and homely be:
Hearth-fire, white cheese, own roof-tree,
True mead slow brewed with brown malt;
But a good woman is savour and salt.

Plow, shove deep through gray loam;
Hack, sword, hack for straw-thatch home;
Guard, buckler, guard both beast and human —
God, send true man his true woman!

Willard Wattles

THE INTERPRETER

IN the very early morning when the light was low
She got all together and she went like snow,
Like snow in the springtime on a sunny hill,
And we were only frightened and can't think still.

We can't think quite that the katydids and frogs
And the little crying chickens and the little grunting
    hogs,
And the other living things that she spoke for to us
Have nothing more to tell her since it happened thus.

She never is around for any one to touch,
But of ecstasy and longing she too knew much,
And always when any one has time to call his own
She will come and be beside him as quiet as a stone.

Orrick Johns

OLD KING COLE [1]

IN Tilbury Town did Old King Cole
A wise old age anticipate,
Desiring, with his pipe and bowl,
No Khan's extravagant estate.
No crown annoyed his honest head,
No fiddlers three were called or needed;
For two disastrous heirs instead
Made music more than ever three did.

[1] Reprinted, by permission of the publishers, from *The Man Against the Sky*, by Edwin Arlington Robinson. Copyright, 1916, by The Macmillan Company.

Bereft of her with whom his life
Was harmony without a flaw,
He took no other for a wife,
Nor sighed for any that he saw;
And if he doubted his two sons,
And heirs, Alexis and Evander,
He might have been as doubtful once
Of Robert Burns and Alexander.

Alexis, in his early youth,
Began to steal — from old and young.
Likewise Evander, and the truth
Was like a bad taste on his tongue.
Born thieves and liars, their affair
Seemed only to be tarred with evil —
The most insufferable pair
Of scamps that ever cheered the devil.

The world went on, their fame went on,
And they went on — from bad to worse;
Till, goaded hot with nothing done,
And each accoutred with a curse,
The friends of Old King Cole, by twos,
And fours, and sevens, and elevens,
Pronounced unalterable views
Of doings that were not of heaven's.

And having learned again whereby
Their baleful zeal had come about,
King Cole met many a wrathful eye
So kindly that its wrath went out —
Or partly out. Say what they would,
He seemed the more to court their candor;

But never told what kind of good
Was in Alexis and Evander.

And Old King Cole, with many a puff
That haloed his urbanity,
Would smoke till he had smoked enough,
And listen most attentively.
He beamed as with an inward light
That had the Lord's assurance in it;
And once a man was there all night,
Expecting something every minute.

But whether from too little thought,
Or too much fealty to the bowl,
A dim reward was all he got
For sitting up with Old King Cole.
"Though mine," the father mused aloud,
"Are not the sons I would have chosen,
Shall I, less evilly endowed,
By their infirmity be frozen?

"They'll have a bad end, I'll agree,
But I was never born to groan;
For I can see what I can see,
And I'm accordingly alone.
With open heart and open door,
I love my friends, I like my neighbors;
But if I try to tell you more,
Your doubts will overmatch my labors.

"This pipe would never make me calm,
This bowl my grief would never drown.
For grief like mine there is no balm
In Gilead, or in Tilbury Town.

And if I see what I can see,
I know not any way to blind it;
Nor more if any way may be
For you to grope or fly to find it.

"There may be room for ruin yet,
And ashes for a wasted love;
Or, like One whom you may forget,
I may have meat you know not of.
And if I'd rather live than weep
Meanwhile, do you find that surprising?
Why, bless my soul, the man's asleep!
That's good. The sun will soon be rising."

Edwin Arlington Robinson

SPOON RIVER ANTHOLOGY [1]

WASHINGTON McNEELY

RICH, honored by my fellow citizens,
The father of many children, born of a noble mother,
All raised there
In the great mansion-house, at the edge of town.
Note the cedar tree on the lawn!
I sent all the boys to Ann Arbor, all of the girls to
    Rockford,
The while my life went on, getting more riches and
    honors —
Resting under my cedar tree at evening.
The years went on.
I sent the girls to Europe;
I dowered them when married.

[1] Reprinted. by permission of the publishers, from *Spoon River Anthology*, by Edgar Lee Masters. Copyright, 1915, by The Macmillan Company.

I gave the boys money to start in business.
They were strong children, promising as apples
Before the bitten places show.
But John fled the country in disgrace.
Jenny died in child-birth —
I sat under my cedar tree.
Harry killed himself after a debauch,
Susan was divorced —
I sat under my cedar tree.
Paul was invalided from over study,
Mary became a recluse at home for love of a man —
I sat under my cedar tree.
All were gone, or broken-winged or devoured by life —
I sat under my cedar tree.
My mate, the mother of them, was taken —
I sat under my cedar tree,
Till ninety years were tolled.
O maternal Earth, which rocks the fallen leaf to sleep!

HARMON WHITNEY

OUT of the lights and roar of cities,
Drifting down like a spark in Spoon River,
Burnt out with the fire of drink, and broken,
The paramour of a woman I took in self-contempt,
But to hide a wounded pride as well.
To be judged and loathed by a village of little minds —
I, gifted with tongues and wisdom,
Sunk here to the dust of the justice court,
A picker of rags in the rubbage of spites and wrongs, —
I, whom fortune smiled on! I in a village,
Spouting to gaping yokels pages of verse,
Out of the lore of golden years,
Or raising a laugh with a flash of filthy wit

When they brought the drinks to kindle my dying
        mind.
To be judged by you,
The soul of me hidden from you,
With its wound gangrened
By love for a wife who made the wound,
With her cold white bosom, treasonous, pure and hard,
Relentless to the last, when the touch of her hand
At any time, might have cured me of the typhus,
Caught in the jungle of life where many are lost.
And only to think that my soul could not react,
As Bryon's did, in song, in something noble,
But turned on itself like a tortured snake —
Judge me this way, O world!

THOMAS TREVELYAN

READING in Ovid the sorrowful story of Itys,
Son of the love of Tereus and Procne, slain
For the guilty passion of Tereus for Philomela,
The flesh of him served to Tereus by Procne,
And the wrath of Tereus, the murderess pursuing
Till the gods made Philomela a nightingale,
Lute of the rising moon, and Procne a swallow!
Oh livers and artists of Hellas centuries gone,
Sealing in little thuribles dreams and wisdom,
Incense beyond all price, forever fragrant,
A breath whereof makes clear the eyes of the soul!
How I inhaled its sweetness here in Spoon River!
The thurible opening when I had lived and learned
How all of us kill the children of love, and all of us,
Knowing not what we do, devour their flesh;
And all of us change to singers, although it be
But once in our lives, or change — alas — to swallows,
To twitter amid cold winds and falling leaves!

ALEXANDER THROCKMORTON

In youth my wings were strong and tireless,
But I did not know the mountains.
In age I knew the mountains
But my weary wings could not follow my vision —
Genius is wisdom and youth.

RUTHERFORD McDOWELL

They brought me ambrotypes
Of the old pioneers to enlarge.
And sometimes one sat for me —
Some one who was in being
When giant hands from the womb of the world
Tore the republic.
What was it in their eyes? —
For I could never fathom
That mystical pathos of drooped eyelids,
And the serene sorrow of their eyes.
It was like a pool of water,
Amid oak trees at the edge of a forest,
Where the leaves fall,
As you hear the crow of a cock
Where the third generation lives, and the strong
        men
From a far-off farm-house, seen near the hills
And the strong women are gone and forgotten.
And these grand-children and great grand-children
Of the pioneers!
Truly did my camera record their faces, too,
With so much of the old strength gone,
And the old faith gone,
And the old mastery of life gone,
And the old courage gone,

Which labors and loves and suffers and sings
Under the sun!

WILLIAM H. HERNDON

THERE by the window in the old house
Perched on the bluff, overlooking miles of valley,
My days of labor closed, sitting out life's decline,
Day by day did I look in my memory,
As one who gazes in an enchantress' crystal globe,
And I saw the figures of the past,
As if in a pageant glassed by a shining dream,
Move through the incredible sphere of time.
And I saw a man arise from the soil like a fabled
        giant
And throw himself over a deathless destiny,
Master of great armies, head of the republic,
Bringing together into a dithyramb of recreative song
The epic hopes of a people;
At the same time Vulcan of sovereign fires,
Where imperishable shields and swords were beaten
        out
From spirits tempered in heaven.
Look in the crystal! See how he hastens on
To the place where his path comes up to the path
Of a child of Plutarch and Shakespeare.
O Lincoln, actor indeed, playing well your part,
And Booth, who strode in a mimic play within the
        play,
Often and often I saw you,
As the cawing crows winged their way to the wood
Over my house-top at solemn sunsets,
There by my window,
Alone.

ANNE RUTLEDGE

OUT of me unworthy and unknown
The vibrations of deathless music:
"With malice toward none, with charity for all."
Out of me the forgiveness of millions toward millions,
And the beneficent face of a nation
Shining with justice and truth.
I am Anne Rutledge who sleep beneath these weeds,
Beloved in life of Abraham Lincoln,
Wedded to him, not through union,
But through separation.
Bloom forever, O Republic,
From the dust of my bosom!

Edgar Lee Masters

LINCOLN

I

LIKE a gaunt, scraggly pine
Which lifts its head above the mournful sandhills;
And patiently, through dull years of bitter silence,
Untended and uncared for, starts to grow.

Ungainly, labouring, huge,
The wind of the north has twisted and gnarled its
    branches;
Yet in the heat of midsummer days, when thunder-
    clouds ring the horizon,
A nation of men shall rest beneath its shade.
And it shall protect them all,
Hold everyone safe there, watching aloof in silence;
Until at last one mad stray bolt from the zenith
Shall strike it in an instant down to earth.

II

There was a darkness in this man; an immense and
hollow darkness,
Of which we may not speak, nor share with him, nor
enter;
A darkness through which strong roots stretched down-
wards into the earth
Towards old things:

Towards the herdman-kings who walked the earth
and spoke with God,
Towards the wanderers who sought for they knew not
what, and found their goal at last;
Towards the men who waited, only waited patiently
when all seemed lost,
Many bitter winters of defeat;

Down to the granite of patience
These roots swept, knotted fibrous roots, prying,
piercing, seeking,
And drew from the living rock and the living waters
about it
The red sap to carry upwards to the sun.

Not proud, but humble,
Only to serve and pass on, to endure to the end
through service;
For the ax is laid at the roots of the trees, and all that
bring not forth good fruit
Shall be cut down on the day to come and cast into
the fire.

III

There is a silence abroad in the land to-day,
And in the hearts of men, a deep and anxious silence;
And, because we are still at last, those bronze lips
    slowly open,
Those hollow and weary eyes take on a gleam of light.

Slowly a patient, firm-syllabled voice cuts through
    the endless silence
Like labouring oxen that drag a plow through the
    chaos of rude clay-fields:
"I went forward as the light goes forward in early
    spring,
But there were also many things which I left behind.

"Tombs that were quiet;
One, of a mother, whose brief light went out in the
    darkness,
One, of a loved one, the snow on whose grave is long
    falling,
One, only of a child, but it was mine.

"Have you forgot your graves? Go, question them in
    anguish,
Listen long to their unstirred lips. From your hostages
    to silence,
Learn there is no life without death, no dawn without
    sun-setting,
No victory but to him who has given all."

IV

The clamour of cannon dies down, the furnace-mouth
    of the battle is silent.

The midwinter sun dips and descends, the earth takes
     on afresh its bright colours.
But he whom we mocked and obeyed not, he whom
     we scorned and mistrusted,
He has descended, like a god, to his rest.

Over the uproar of cities,
Over the million intricate threads of life wavering and
     crossing,
In the midst of problems we know not, tangling, per-
     plexing, ensnaring,   .
Rises one white tomb alone.

Beam over it, stars,
Wrap it round, stripes — stripes red for the pain that
     he bore for you —
Enfold it forever, O flag, rent, soiled, but repaired
     through your anguish;
Long as you keep him there safe, the nations shall bow
     to your law.

Strew over him flowers:
Blue forget-me-nots from the north, and the bright
     pink arbutus
From the east, and from the west rich orange blos-
     som,
And from the heart of the land take the passion-
     flower;

Rayed, violet, dim,
With the nails that pierced, the cross that he bore and
     the circlet,

And beside it there lay also one lonely snow-white
    magnolia,
Bitter for remembrance of the healing which has
    passed.

John Gould Fletcher

ABRAHAM LINCOLN WALKS AT MIDNIGHT[1]

IT is portentous, and a thing of state
That here at midnight, in our little town
A mourning figure walks, and will not rest,
Near the old court-house pacing up and down,

Or by his homestead, or in shadowed yards
He lingers where his children used to play,
Or through the market, on the well-worn stones
He stalks until the dawn-stars burn away.

A bronzed, lank man! His suit of ancient black,
A famous high-top hat and plain worn shawl
Make him the quaint great figure that men love,
The prairie lawyer, master of us all.

He cannot sleep upon his hillside now.
He is among us: — as in times before!
And we who toss and lie awake for long
Breathe deep, and start, to see him pass the door.

His head is bowed. He thinks on men and kings.
Yea, when the sick world cries, how can he sleep?

[1] Reprinted, by permission of the publishers, from *The Congo, and Other Poems*, by Vachel Lindsay. Copyright, 1914, by The Macmillan Company.

Too many peasants fight, they know not why,
Too many homesteads in black terror weep.

The sins of all the war-lords burn his heart.
He sees the dreadnaughts scouring every main.
He carries on his shawl-wrapped shoulders now
The bitterness, the folly and the pain.

He cannot rest until a spirit-dawn
Shall come; — the shining hope of Europe free:
The league of sober folk, the Workers' Earth,
Bringing long peace to Cornland, Alp and Sea.

It breaks his heart that kings must murder still,
That all his hours of travail here for men
Seem yet in vain. And who will bring white peace
That he may sleep upon his hill again?

Vachel Lindsay

PRAYER DURING BATTLE

LORD, in this hour of tumult,
　　Lord, in this night of fears,
Keep open, oh, keep open
　　My eyes, my ears.

Not blindly, not in hatred,
　　Lord, let me do my part.
Keep open, oh, keep open
　　My mind, my heart!

Hermann Hagedorn

PRAYER OF A SOLDIER IN FRANCE

My shoulders ache beneath my pack
(Lie easier, Cross, upon His back).

I march with feet that burn and smart
(Tread, Holy Feet, upon my heart).

Men shout at me who may not speak
(They scourged Thy back and smote Thy cheek).

I may not lift a hand to clear
My eyes of salty drops that sear.

(Then shall my fickle soul forget
Thy Agony of Bloody Sweat?)

My rifle hand is stiff and numb
(From Thy pierced palm red rivers come).

Lord, Thou didst suffer more for me
Than all the hosts of land and sea.

So let me render back again
This millionth of Thy gift. Amen.

Joyce Kilmer

THE WHITE COMRADE

Under our curtain of fire,
Over the clotted clods,
We charged, to be withered, to reel
And despairingly wheel
When the bugles bade us retire
From the terrible odds.

As we ebbed with the battle-tide,
Fingers of red-hot steel
Suddenly closed on my side.
I fell, and began to pray.
I crawled on my hands and lay
Where a shallow crater yawned wide;
Then I swooned. . . .

When I woke, it was yet day.
Fierce was the pain of my wound,
But I saw it was death to stir,
For fifty paces away
Their trenches were.
In torture I prayed for the dark
And the stealthy step of my friend
Who, stanch to the very end,
Would creep to the danger zone
And offer his life as a mark
To save my own.

Night fell. I heard his tread,
Not stealthy, but firm and serene,
As if my comrade's head
Were lifted far from that scene
Of passion and pain and dread;
As if my comrade's heart
In carnage took no part;
As if my comrade's feet
Were set on some radiant street
Such as no darkness might haunt;
As if my comrade's eyes,
No deluge of flame could surprise,
No death and destruction daunt,

No red-beaked bird dismay,
Nor sight of decay.

Then in the bursting shells' dim light
I saw he was clad in white.
For a moment I thought that I saw the smock
Of a shepherd in search of his flock.
Alert were the enemy, too,
And their bullets flew
Straight at a mark no bullet could fail;
For the seeker was tall and his robe was bright;
But he did not flee nor quail.
Instead, with unhurrying stride
He came,
And gathering my tall frame,
Like a child, in his arms . . .

I slept,
And awoke
From a blissful dream
In a cave by a stream.
My silent comrade had bound my side.
No pain now was mine, but a wish that I spoke, —
A mastering wish to serve this man
Who had ventured through hell my doom to revoke,
As only the truest of comrades can.
I begged him to tell me how best I might aid him,
And urgently prayed him
Never to leave me, whatever betide;
When I saw he was hurt —
Shot through the hands that were clasped in prayer!
Then, as the dark drops gathered there
And fell in the dirt,

The wounds of my friend
Seemed to me such as no man might bear.
Those bullet-holes in the patient hands
Seemed to transcend
All horrors that ever these war-drenched lands
Had known or would know till the mad world's end.
Then suddenly I was aware
That his feet had been wounded, too;
And, dimming the white of his side,
A dull stain grew.
"You are hurt, White Comrade!" I cried.
His words I already foreknew:
"These are old wounds," said he,
"But of late they have troubled me."

Robert Haven Schauffler

SMITH, OF THE THIRD OREGON, DIES [1]

AUTUMN in Oregon is wet as Spring,
And green, with little singings in the grass,
    And pheasants flying,
Gold, green and red,
Great, narrow, lovely things,
As if an orchid had snatched wings.
There are strange birds like blots against a sky
    Where a sun is dying.
Beyond the river where the hills are blurred
A cloud, like the one word
Of the too-silent sky, stirs, and there stand
    Black trees on either hand.

[1] Reprinted, by permission of the publishers, from *Drums in Our Street*, by Mary Carolyn Davies. Copyright. 1918, by the Macmillan Company.

Autumn in Oregon is wet and new
    As Spring,
And puts a fever like Spring's in the cheek
That once has touched her dew —
And it puts longing too
In eyes that once have seen
Her season-flouting green,
    And ears that listened to her strange birds
      speak.

Autumn in Oregon — I'll never see
Those hills again, a blur of blue and rain
Across the old Willamette. I'll not stir
A pheasant as I walk, and hear it whirr
Above my head, an indolent, trusting thing.
When all this silly dream is finished here,
The fellows will go home to where there fall
Rose-petals over every street, and all
The year is like a friendly festival.
But I shall never watch those hedges drip
Color, not see the tall spar of a ship
In our old harbor. — They say that I am dying,
Perhaps that's why it all comes back again:
Autumn in Oregon and pheasants flying —
               Mary Carolyn Davies

SONG

    SHE goes all so softly
      Like a shadow on the hill,
    A faint wind at twilight
      That stirs, and is still.

She weaves her thoughts whitely,
   Like doves in the air,
Though a gray mound in Flanders
   Clouds all that was fair.

                 Edward J. O'Brien

LONELY BURIAL

THERE were not many at that lonely place,
Where two scourged hills met in a little plain.
The wind cried loud in gusts, then low again.
Three pines strained darkly, runners in a race
Unseen by any. Toward the further woods
A dim harsh noise of voices rose and ceased.
— We were most silent in those solitudes —
Then, sudden as a flame, the black-robed priest,
The clotted earth piled roughly up about
The hacked red oblong of the new-made thing,
Short words in swordlike Latin — and a rout
Of dreams most impotent, unwearying.
Then, like a blind door shut on a carouse,
The terrible bareness of the soul's last house.

                Stephen Vincent Benét

I HAVE A RENDEZVOUS WITH DEATH

I HAVE a rendezvous with Death
At some disputed barricade,
When Spring comes back with rustling shade
And apple-blossoms fill the air —
I have a rendezvous with Death
When Spring brings back blue days and fair.

It may be he shall take my hand
And lead me into his dark land
And close my eyes and quench my breath —
It may be I shall pass him still.
I have a rendezvous with Death
On some scarred slope of battered hill
When Spring comes round again this year
And the first meadow-flowers appear.

God knows 't were better to be deep
Pillowed in silk and scented down,
Where Love throbs out in blissful sleep,
Pulse nigh to pulse, and breath to breath,
Where hushed awakenings are dear . . .
But I've a rendezvous with Death
At midnight in some flaming town,
When Spring trips north again this year,
And I to my pledged word am true,
I shall not fail that rendezvous.

Alan Seeger

ROUGE BOUQUET

In a wood they call the Rouge Bouquet
There is a new-made grave to-day,
Built by never a spade nor pick
Yet covered with earth ten metres thick.
There lie many fighting men,
   Dead in their youthful prime,
Never to laugh nor love again
   Nor taste the Summertime.
For Death came flying through the air
And stopped his flight at the dugout stair,

Touched his prey and left them there,
  Clay to clay.
He hid their bodies stealthily
In the soil of the land they fought to free
  And fled away.
Now over the grave abrupt and clear
  Three volleys ring;
And perhaps their brave young spirits hear
  The bugle sing:
"Go to sleep!
Go to sleep!
Slumber well where the shell screamed and fell.
Let your rifles rest on the muddy floor,
You will not need them any more.
Danger's past;
Now at last,
Go to sleep!"

There is on earth no worthier grave
To hold the bodies of the brave
Than this place of pain and pride
Where they nobly fought and nobly died.
Never fear but in the skies
Saints and angels stand
Smiling with their holy eyes
On this new-come band.
St. Michael's sword darts through the air
And touches the aureole on his hair
As he sees them stand saluting there,
  His stalwart sons;
And Patrick, Brigid, Columkill
Rejoice that in veins of warriors still
  The Gael's blood runs.

And up to Heaven's doorway floats,
From the wood called Rouge Bouquet,
A delicate cloud of buglenotes
That softly say:
"Farewell!
Farewell!
Comrades true, born anew, peace to you!
Your souls shall be where the heroes are
And your memory shine like the morning-star.
Brave and dear,
Shield us here.
Farewell!"

Joyce Kilmer

FRANCIS LEDWIDGE

(*Killed in action July 31, 1917*)

NEVERMORE singing
Will you go now,
Wearing wild moonlight
On your brow.
The moon's white mood
In your silver mind
Is all forgotten.
Words of wind
From off the hedgerow
After rain,
You do not hear them;
They are vain.
There is a linnet
Craves a song,
And you returning
Before long.

Now who will tell her,
Who can say
On what great errand
You are away?
You whose kindred
Were hills of Meath,
Who sang the lane-rose
From her sheath,
What voice will cry them
The grief at dawn
Or say to the blackbird
You are gone?

Grace Hazard Conkling

APRIL ON THE BATTLEFIELDS

APRIL now walks the fields again,
Trailing her tearful leaves
And holding all her frightened buds against her heart:
Wrapt in her clouds and mists,
She walks,
Groping her way among the graves of men.

The green of earth is differently green,
A dreadful knowledge trembles in the grass,
And little wide-eyed flowers die too soon:
There is a stillness here —
After a terror of all raving sounds —
And birds sit close for comfort upon the boughs
Of broken trees.

April, thou grief!
What of thy sun and glad, high wind,

Thy valiant hills and woods and eager brooks,
Thy thousand-petalled hopes?
The sky forbids thee sorrow, April!
And yet —
I see thee walking listlessly
Across those scars that once were joyous sod,
Those graves,
Those stepping-stones from life to life.

Death is an interruption between two heart-beats,
That I know —
Yet know not how I know —
But April mourns,
Trailing her tender green,
The passion of her green,
Across the passion of those fearful fields.

Yes, all the fields
No barrier here,
No challenge in the night,
No stranger-land;
She passes with her perfect countersign,
Her green;
She wanders in her mournful garden,
Dropping her buds like tears,
Spreading her lovely grief upon the graves of man.
Leonora Speyer

EARTH'S EASTER
(1915)

EARTH has gone up from its Gethsemane,
And now on Golgotha is crucified;
The spear is twisted in the tortured side;
The thorny crown still works its cruelty.

Hark! while the victim suffers on the tree,
  There sound through starry spaces, far and wide,
  Such words as in the last despair are cried:
"My God! my God! Thou hast forsaken me!"

But when earth's members from the cross are drawn,
And all we love into the grave is gone,
  This hope shall be a spark within the gloom:
That, in the glow of some stupendous dawn,
  We may go forth to find, where lilies bloom,
  Two angels bright before an empty tomb.
                    Robert Haven Schauffler

THE FIELDS

THOUGH wisdom underfoot
  Dies in the bloody fields,
Slowly the endless root
  Gathers again and yields.

In fields where hate has hurled
  Its force, where folly rots,
Wisdom shall be unfurled
  Small as forget-me-nots.
                    Witter Bynner

IN SPITE OF WAR

IN spite of war, in spite of death,
In spite of all man's sufferings,
Something within me laughs and sings
And I must praise with all my breath.
In spite of war, in spite of hate
Lilacs are blooming at my gate,

Tulips are tripping down the path
In spite of war, in spite of wrath.
"Courage!" the morning-glory saith;
"Rejoice!" the daisy murmureth,
And just to live is so divine
When pansies lift their eyes to mine.

The clouds are romping with the sea,
And flashing waves call back to me
That naught is real but what is fair,
That everywhere and everywhere
A glory liveth through despair.
Though guns may roar and cannon boom,
Roses are born and gardens bloom;
My spirit still may light its flame
At that same torch whence poppies came.
Where morning's altar whitely burns
Lilies may lift their silver urns
In spite of war, in spite of shame.

And in my ear a whispering breath,
"Wake from the nightmare! Look and see
That life is naught but ecstasy
In spite of war, in spite of death!"

Angela Morgan

WIDE HAVEN

TIRED of man's futile, petty cry,
  Of lips that lie and flout,
I saw the slow sun dim and die
  And the slim dusk slip out . . .
Life held no room for doubt.

What though Death claim the ones I prize
  In War's insane crusade,
Last night I saw Orion rise
  And the great day-star fade,
  And I am not dismayed.

Clement Wood

TO ANY ONE

WHETHER the time be slow or fast,
  Enemies, hand in hand,
Must come together at the last
  And understand.

No matter how the die is cast
  Nor who may seem to win,
You know that you must love at last —
  Why not begin?

Witter Bynner

PEACE

SUDDENLY bells and flags!
Suddenly — door to door —
Tidings! Can we believe,
We, who were used to war?

Yet we have dreamed her face,
Knowing her light must be,
Knowing that she must come.
Look — she comes, it is she!

Tattered her raiment floats,
Blood is upon her wings.

Ah, but her eyes are clear!
Ah, but her voice outrings!

Soon where the shrapnel fell
Petals shall wake and stir.
Look — she is here, she lives!
Beauty has died for her.

Agnes Lee

THE KINGS ARE PASSING DEATHWARD

THE Kings are passing deathward in the dark
  Of days that had been splendid where they went;
Their crowns are captive and their courts are stark
  Of purples that are ruinous, now, and rent.
For all that they have seen disastrous things:
  The shattered pomp, the split and shaken throne,
They cannot quite forget the way of Kings:
  Gravely they pass, majestic and alone.

With thunder on their brows, their faces set
  Toward the eternal night of restless shapes,
They walk in awful splendor, regal yet,
  Wearing their crimes like rich and kingly capes . . .
Curse them or taunt, they will not hear or see;
  The Kings are passing deathward: let them be.

David Morton

JERICO

JERICO, Jerico,
Round and round the walls I go
Where they watch with scornful eyes,
Where the captained bastions rise;

Heel and toe, heel and toe,
Blithely round the walls I go.

Jerico, Jerico,
Round and round the walls I go . . .
All the golden ones of earth
Regal in their lordly mirth . . .
Heel and toe, heel and toe,
Round and round the walls I go.

Jerico, Jerico,
Blithely round the walls I go,
With a broken sword in hand
Where the mighty bastions stand;
Heel and toe, heel and toe,
Hear my silly bugle blow.

Heel and toe, heel and toe,
Round the walls of Jerico . . .
Past the haughty golden gate
Where the emperor in state
Smiles to see the ragged show,
Round and round the towers go.

Jerico, Jerico,
Round and round and round I go . . .
All their sworded bodies must
Lie low in their tower's dust . . .
Heel and toe, heel and toe,
Blithely round the walls I go.

Heel and toe, heel and toe, —
I will blow a thunder note

From my brazen bugle's throat
Till the sand and thistle know
The leveled walls of Jerico,
Jerico, Jerico, Jerico, . . .

Willard Wattles

STUDENTS

JOHN BROWN and Jeanne at Fontainebleau —
'T was Toussaint, just a year ago;
Crimson and copper was the glow
Of all the woods at Fontainebleau.
They peered into that ancient well,
And watched the slow torch as it fell.
John gave the keeper two whole sous,
And Jeanne that smile with which she woos
John Brown to folly. So they lose
The Paris train. But never mind! —
All-Saints are rustling in the wind,
And there's an inn, a crackling fire —
(It's *deux-cinquante*, but Jeanne's desire);
There's dinner, candles, country wine,
Jeanne's lips — philosophy divine!

There was a bosquet at Saint Cloud
Wherein John's picture of her grew
To be a Salon masterpiece —
Till the rain fell that would not cease.
Through one long alley how they raced! —
'T was gold and brown, and all a waste
Of matted leaves, moss-interlaced.
Shades of mad queens and hunter-kings
And thorn-sharp feet of dryad-things

Were company to their wanderings;
Then rain and darkness on them drew.
The rich folks' motors honked and flew.
They hailed an old cab, heaven for two;
The bright Champs-Elysées at last —
Though the cab crawled it sped too fast.

Paris, upspringing white and gold:
Flamboyant arch and high-enscrolled
War-sculpture, big, Napoleonic —
Fierce chargers, angels histrionic;
The royal sweep of gardened spaces,
The pomp and whirl of columned Places;
The *Rive Gauche*, age-old, gay and gray;
The *impasse* and the loved café;
The tempting tidy little shops;
The convent walls, the glimpsed tree-tops;
Book-stalls, old men like dwarfs in plays;
Talk, work, and Latin Quarter ways.

May — Robinson's, the chestnut trees —
Were ever crowds as gay as these?
The quick pale waiters on a run,
The round, green tables, one by one,
Hidden away in amorous bowers —
Lilac, laburnum's golden showers.
Kiss, clink of glasses, laughter heard,
And nightingales quite undeterred.
And then that last extravagance —
O Jeanne, a single amber glance
Will pay him! — "Let's play millionaire
For just two hours — on princely fare,

At some hotel where lovers dine
À *deux* and pledge across the wine!"
They find a damask breakfast-room,
Where stiff silk roses range their bloom.
The *garcon* has a splendid way
Of bearing in *grand déjeuner.*
Then to be left alone, alone,
High up above Rue Castiglione;
Curtained away from all the rude
Rumors, in silken solitude;
And, John, her head upon your knees —
Time waits for moments such as these.

Florence Wilkinson

TAMPICO

OH, cut me reeds to blow upon,
　Or gather me a star,
But leave the sultry passion-flowers
　Growing where they are.

I fear their sombre yellow deeps,
　Their whirling fringe of black,
And he who gives a passion-flower
　Always asks it back.

Grace Hazard Conkling

WHICH

WE ask that Love shall rise to the divine,
And yet we crave him very human, too;
Our hearts would drain the crimson of his wine,
Our souls despise him if he prove untrue!

Poor Love! I hardly see what you can do!
We know all human things are weak and frail,
And yet we claim that very part of you,
Then, inconsistent, blame you if you fail.
When you would soar, 't is we who clip your wings,
Although we weep because you faint and fall.
Alas! it seems we want so many things,
That no dear love could ever grant them all!
Which shall we choose, the human or divine,
The crystal stream, or yet the crimson wine?

Corinne Roosevelt Robinson

APOLOGY [1]

BE not angry with me that I bear
     Your colours everywhere,
     All through each crowded street,
         And meet
     The wonder-light in every eye,
         As I go by.

Each plodding wayfarer looks up to gaze,
     Blinded by rainbow haze,
     The stuff of happiness,
         No less,
     Which wraps me in its glad-hued folds
         Of peacock golds.

Before my feet the dusty, rough-paved way
     Flushes beneath its gray.

[1] Reprinted, by permission of the publishers, from *Sword Blades and Poppy Seed,* by Amy Lowell. Copyright, 1914, by The Macmillan Company.

My steps fall ringed with light,
        So bright,
It seems a myriad suns are strown
        About the town.

Around me is the sound of steepled bells,
        And rich perfuméd smells
Hang like a wind-forgotten cloud,
        And shroud
Me from close contact with the world.
        I dwell impearled.

You blazen me with jewelled insignia.
        A flaming nebula
Rims in my life. And yet
        You set
The word upon me, unconfessed
        To go unguessed.

                              Amy Lowell

THE GREAT HUNT

I CANNOT tell you now;
        When the wind's drive and whirl
        Blow me along no longer,
        And the wind's a whisper at last —
Maybe I'll tell you then —

                some other time.

        When the rose's flash to the sunset
        Reels to the wrack and the twist,
        And the rose is a red bygone,
        When the face I love is going

And the gate to the end shall clang,
And it's no use to beckon or say, "So long" —
Maybe I'll tell you then —
> some other time.

I never knew any more beautiful than you:
I have hunted you under my thoughts,
I have broken down under the wind
And into the roses looking for you.
I shall never find any
> greater than you.
>> *Carl Sandburg*

DIALOGUE

BE patient, Life, when Love is at the gate,
And when he enters let him be at home.
Think of the roads that he has had to roam.
Think of the years that he has had to wait.

But if I let Love in I shall be late.
Another has come first — there is no room.
And I am thoughtful of the endless loom —
Let Love be patient, the importunate.

O Life, be idle and let Love come in,
And give thy dreamy hair that Love may spin.

But Love himself is idle with his song.
Let Love come last, and then may Love last long.

Be patient, Life, for Love is not the last.
Be patient now with Death, for Love has passed.
> *Walter Conrad Arensberg*

SONG

The Spring will come when the year turns,
  As if no Winter had been,
But what shall I do with a locked heart
  That lets no new year in?

The birds will go when the Fall goes,
  The leaves will fade in the field,
But what shall I do with an old love
  Will neither die nor yield?

Oh! youth will turn as the world turns,
  And dim grow laughter and pain,
But how shall I hide from an old dream
  I never may dream again?

Margaret Widdemer

THE BITTER HERB

O bitter herb, Forgetfulness,
I search for you in vain;
You are the only growing thing
Can take away my pain.

When I was young, this bitter herb
Grew wild on every hill;
I should have plucked a store of it,
And kept it by me still.

I hunt through all the meadows
Where once I wandered free,
But the rare herb, Forgetfulness,
It hides away from me.

O bitter herb, Forgetfulness,
Where is your drowsy breath?
Oh, can it be your seed has blown
Far as the Vales of Death?

Jeanne Robert Foster

BEHIND THE HOUSE IS THE MILLET PLOT

BEHIND the house is the millet plot,
And past the millet, the stile;
And then a hill where melilot
Grows with wild camomile.

There was a youth who bade me goodby
Where the hill rises to meet the sky.
I think my heart broke; but I have forgot
All but the smell of the white melilot.

Muna Lee

MEN OF HARLAN

HERE in the level country, where the creeks run
    straight and wide,
Six men upon their pacing nags may travel side by
    side.
But the mountain men of Harlan, you may tell them
    all the while,
When they pass through our village, for they ride in
    single file.
And the children, when they see them, stop their play
    and stand and cry,
"Here come the men of Harlan, men of Harlan, riding
    by!"

O the mountain men of Harlan, when they come down
    to the plain,
With dangling stirrup, jangling spur, and loosely
    hanging rein,
They do not ride, like our folks here, in twos and
    threes abreast,
With merry laughter, talk and song, and lightly spoken
    jest;
But silently and solemnly, in long and straggling line,
As you may see them in the hills, beyond Big Black
    and Pine.

For, in that far strange country, where the men of
    Harlan dwell,
There are no roads at all, like ours, as we've heard
    travelers tell.
But only narrow trails that wind along each shallow
    creek,
Where the silence hangs so heavy, you can hear the
    leathers squeak.
And there no two can ride abreast, but each alone
    must go,
Picking his way as best he may, with careful steps and
    slow,

Down many a shelving ledge of shale, skirting the
    trembling sands,
Through many a pool and many a pass, where the
    mountain laurel stands
So thick and close to left and right, with holly bushes,
    too,
The clinging branches meet midway to bar the passage
    through, —

O'er many a steep and stony ridge, o'er many a high
  divide,
And so it is the Harlan men thus one by one do ride.

Yet it is strange to see them pass in line through our
  wide street,
When they come down to sell their sang, and buy their
  stores of meat,
These silent men, in sombre black, all clad from foot
  to head,
Though they have left their lonely hills and the narrow creek's rough bed.
And 't is no wonder children stop their play and stand
  and cry:
"Here come the men of Harlan, men of Harlan, riding
  by."

William Aspinwall Bradley

HAVE YOU AN EYE

HAVE you an eye for the trails, the trails,
  The old mark and the new?
What scurried here, what loitered there,
  In the dust and in the dew?

Have you an eye for the beaten track,
  The old hoof and the young?
Come name me the drivers of yesterday,
  Sing me the songs they sung.

O, was it a schooner last went by,
  And where will it ford the stream?
Where will it halt in the early dusk,
  And where will the camp-fire gleam?

They used to take the shortest cut
    The cattle trails had made;
Get down the hill by the easy slope
    .To the water and the shade.

But it's barbed wire fence, and section line,
    And kill-horse travel now;
Scoot you down the canyon bank, —
    The old road 's under plough.

Have you an eye for the laden wheel,
    The worn tire or the new?
Or the sign of the prairie pony's hoof
    Was never trimmed for shoe?
                      Edwin Ford Piper

AFTER APPLE-PICKING

My long two-pointed ladder 's sticking through a tree
Toward heaven still,
And there's a barrel that I did n't fill
Beside it, and there may be two or three
Apples I did n't pick upon some bough.
But I am done with apple-picking now.
Essence of winter sleep is on the night,
The scent of apples: I am drowsing off.
I cannot rub the strangeness from my sight
I got from looking through a pane of glass
I skimmed this morning from the drinking trough
And held against the world of hoary grass.
It melted, and I let it fall and break.
But I was well
Upon my way to sleep before it fell,
And I could tell

What form my dreaming was about to take.
Magnified apples appear and disappear,
Stem end and blossom end,
And every fleck of russet showing clear.
My instep arch not only keeps the ache,
It keeps the pressure of a ladder-round.
I feel the ladder sway as the boughs bend.
And I keep hearing from the cellar bin
The rumbling sound
Of load on load of apples coming in.
For I have had too much
Of apple-picking: I am overtired
Of the great harvest I myself desired.
There were ten thousand thousand fruit to touch,
Cherish in hand, lift down, and not let fall.
For all
That struck the earth,
No matter if not bruised or spiked with stubble,
Went surely to the cider-apple heap
As of no worth.
One can see what will trouble
This sleep of mine, whatever sleep it is.
Were he not gone,
The woodchuck could say whether it's like his
Long sleep, as I describe its coming on,
Or just some human sleep.

Robert Frost

AUTUMN

(*For my Mother*)

How memory cuts away the years,
And how clean the picture comes
Of autumn days, brisk and busy;

Charged with keen sunshine.
And you, stirred with activity;
The spirit of these energetic days.

There was our back-yard,
So plain and stripped of green,
With even the weeds carefully pulled away
From the crooked, red bricks that made the walk.
And the earth on either side so black.

Autumn and dead leaves burning in the sharp air;
And winter comforts coming in like a pageant.
I shall not forget them:
Great jars laden with the raw green of pickles,
Standing in a solemn row across the back of the porch,
Exhaling the pungent dill;
And in the very center of the yard,
You, tending the great catsup kettle of gleaming
     copper
Where fat, red tomatoes bobbed up and down
Like jolly monks in a drunken dance.
And there were bland banks of cabbages that came by
     the wagon-load,
Soon to be cut into delicate ribbons
Only to be crushed by the heavy, wooden stompers.
Such feathery whiteness — to come to kraut!
And after, there were grapes that hid their brightness
     under a grey dust,
Then gushed thrilling, purple blood over the fire;
And enamelled crab-apples that tricked with their
     fragrance
But were bitter to taste.
And there were spicy plums and ill-shaped quinces,

And long string beans floating in pans of clear water
Like slim, green fishes.
And there was fish itself,
Salted, silver herring from the city . . .

And you moved among these mysteries,
Absorbed and smiling and sure;
Stirring, tasting, measuring,
With the precision of a ritual.
I like to think of you in your years of power —
You, now so shaken and so powerless —
High priestess of your home.

Jean Starr Untermeyer

AUTUMN MOVEMENT

I CRIED over beautiful things knowing no beautiful
thing lasts.

The field of cornflower yellow is a scarf at the neck of
the copper sunburned woman, the mother of
the year, the taker of seeds.

The northwest wind comes and the yellow is torn full
of holes, new beautiful things come in the first
spit of snow on the northwest wind, and the old
things go, not one lasts.

Carl Sandburg

GOD'S WORLD

O WORLD, I cannot hold thee close enough!
Thy winds, thy wide grey skies!
Thy mists that roll and rise!

Thy woods this autumn day, that ache and sag
And all but cry with colour! That gaunt crag
To crush! To lift the lean of that black bluff!
World, World, I cannot get thee close enough!

Long have I known a glory in it all,
But never knew I this;
Here such a passion is
As stretcheth me apart, — Lord, I do fear
Thou'st made the world too beautiful this year;
My soul is all but out of me, — let fall
No burning leaf; prithee, let no bird call.

Edna St. Vincent Millay

OVERTONES

I HEARD a bird at break of day
Sing from the autumn trees
A song so mystical and calm,
So full of certainties,
No man, I think, could listen long
Except upon his knees.
Yet this was but a simple bird,
Alone, among dead trees.

William Alexander Percy

WHEN THE YEAR GROWS OLD

I CANNOT but remember
When the year grows old —
October — November —
How she disliked the cold!

She used to watch the swallows
    Go down across the sky,
And turn from the window
    With a little sharp sigh.

And often when the brown leaves
    Were brittle on the ground,
And the wind in the chimney
    Made a melancholy sound,

She had a look about her
    That I wish I could forget —
The look of a scared thing
    Sitting in a net!

Oh, beautiful at nightfall
    The soft spitting snow!
And beautiful the bare boughs
    Rubbing to and fro!

But the roaring of the fire,
    And the warmth of fur,
And the boiling of the kettle
    Were beautiful to her!

I cannot but remember
    When the year grows old —
October — November —
    How she disliked the cold!

                    Edna St. Vincent Millay

IN THE MONASTERY

COLD is the wind to-night, and rough the sea,
Too rough for even the daring Dane to find
A landing-place upon the frozen lea.
                              Cold is the wind.

The blast sweeps round the chapel from behind,
Making the altar-light flare fitfully,
While I must kneel and pray with troubled mind.

Patrick and Brigid, I have prayed to ye!
The night is over, and my task resigned
To Colum. Though God's own dwelling shelter me,
                              Cold is the wind.
                    Norreys Jephson O'Conor

THE NARROW DOORS

THE Wide Door into Sorrow
Stands open night and day.
With head held high and dancing feet
I pass it on my way.

I never tread within it,
I never turn to see
The Wide Door into Sorrow.
It cannot frighten me.

The Narrow Doors to Sorrow
Are secret, still, and low:
Swift tongues of dusk that spoil the sun
Before I even know.

My dancing feet are frozen.
I stare. I can but see.
The Narrow Doors to Sorrow
They stop the heart in me.

— Oh, stranger than my midnights
Of loneliness and strife
The Doors that let the dark leap in
Across my sunny life!

Fannie Stearns Davis

I PASS A LIGHTED WINDOW

I PASS a lighted window
    And a closed door —
And I am not troubled
    Any more.

Though the road is murky,
    I am not afraid,
For a shadow passes
    On the lighted shade.

Once I knew the sesame
    To the closed door;
Now I shall not enter
    Any more;

Nor will people passing
    By the lit place,
See our shadows marry
    In a gray embrace.

Strange a passing shadow
Has a long spell!
What can matter, knowing
She does well?

How can life annoy me
Any more?
Life: a lighted window
And a closed door.

Clement Wood

DOORS [1]

LIKE a young child who to his mother's door
Runs eager for the welcoming embrace,
And finds the door shut, and with troubled face
Calls and through sobbing calls, and o'er and o'er
Calling, storms at the panel — so before
A door that will not open, sick and numb,
I listen for a word that will not come,
And know, at last, I may not enter more.

Silence! And through the silence and the dark
By that closed door, the distant sob of tears
Beats on my spirit, as on fairy shores
The spectral sea; and through the sobbing — hark!
Down the fair-chambered corridor of years,
The quiet shutting, one by one, of doors.

Hermann Hagedorn

[1] Reprinted, by permission of the publishers, from *Poems and Ballads* by Hermann Hagedorn. Copyright 1913, by The Macmillan Company.

WHERE LOVE ONCE WAS

WHERE love once was, let there be no hate:
Though they that went as one by night and day
Go now alone,
Where love once was, let there be no hate.

The seeds we planted together
Came to rich harvest,
And our hearts are as bins brimming with the golden
      plenty:
Into our loneliness we carry granaries of old love . . .

And though the time has come when we cannot sow
      our acres together,
And our souls need diverse fields,
And a tilling apart,
Let us go separate ways with a blessing each for each,
And gentle parting,
And let there be no hate,
Where love once was.

James Oppenheim

IRISH LOVE SONG

WELL, if the thing is over, better it is for me,
The lad was ever a rover, loving and laughing free,
Far too clever a lover not to be having still
A lass in the town and a lass by the road and a lass
      by the farther hill —
Love on the field and love on the path and love in the
      woody glen —
(Lad, will I never see you, never your face again?)

Ay, if the thing is ending, now I'll be getting rest,
Saying my prayers and bending down to be stilled and
 blest,
Never the days are sending hope till my heart is
 sore
For a laugh on the path and a voice by the gate and a
 step on the shieling floor —
Grief on my ways and grief on my work and grief till
 the evening's dim —
(Lord, will I never hear it, never a sound of him?)

Sure if it's done forever, better for me that's wise,
Never the hurt, and never tears in my aching eyes,
No more the trouble ever to hide from my asking
 folk
Beat of my heart at click o' the latch, and throb if
 his name is spoke;
Never the need to hide the sighs and the flushing
 thoughts and the fret,
And after awhile my heart will hush and my hungering
 hands forget . . .
Peace on my ways, and peace in my step, and maybe
 my heart grown light —
(*Mary, helper of heartbreak, send him to me to-night!*)

Margaret Widdemer

NIRVANA

SLEEP on — I lie at heaven's high oriels,
 Over the stars that murmur as they go
 Lighting your lattice-window far below;
And every star some of the glory spells
 Whereof I know.

I have forgotten you, long long ago;
    Like the sweet, silver singing of thin bells
Vanished, or music fading faint and low.
    Sleep on — I lie at heaven's high oriels,
Who loved you so.

                John Hall Wheelock

A NUN

ONE glance and I had lost her in the riot
    Of tangled cries.
She trod the clamor with a cloistral quiet
    Deep in her eyes
As though she heard the muted music only
    That silence makes
Among dim mountain summits and on lonely
    Deserted lakes.

There is some broken song her heart remembers
    From long ago,
Some love lies buried deep, some passion's embers
    Smothered in snow,
Far voices of a joy that sought and missed her
    Fail now, and cease . . .
And this has given the deep eyes of God's sister
    Their dreadful peace.

                Odell Shepard

SILENCE [1]

I HAVE known the silence of the stars and of the sea,
And the silence of the city when it pauses,
And the silence of a man and a maid,

[1] Reprinted, by permission of the publishers, from *Songs and Satires*, by Edgar Lee Masters. Copyright, 1915, by The Macmillan Company.

And the silence of the sick
When their eyes roam about the room.
And I ask: For the depths,
Of what use is language?
A beast of the field moans a few times
When death takes its young.
And we are voiceless in the presence of realities —
We cannot speak.

A curious boy asks an old soldier
Sitting in front of the grocery store,
"How did you lose your leg?"
And the old soldier is struck with silence,
Or his mind flies away
Because he cannot concentrate it on Gettysburg.
It comes back jocosely
And he says, "A bear bit it off."
And the boy wonders, while the old soldier
Dumbly, feebly lives over
The flashes of guns, the thunder of cannon,
The shrieks of the slain,
And himself lying on the ground,
And the hospital surgeons, the knives,
And the long days in bed.
But if he could describe it all
He would be an artist.
But if he were an artist there would be deeper
        wounds
Which he could not describe.

There is the silence of a great hatred,
And the silence of a great love,
And the silence of an embittered friendship.

There is the silence of a spiritual crisis,
Through which your soul, exquisitely tortured,
Comes with visions not to be uttered
Into a realm of higher life.
There is the silence of defeat.
There is the silence of those unjustly punished;
And the silence of the dying whose hand
Suddenly grips yours.
There is the silence between father and son,
When the father cannot explain his life,
Even though he be misunderstood for it.

There is the silence that comes between husband and
          wife.
There is the silence of those who have failed;
And the vast silence that covers
Broken nations and vanquished leaders.
There is the silence of Lincoln,
Thinking of the poverty of his youth.
And the silence of Napoleon
After Waterloo.
And the silence of Jeanne d'Arc
Saying amid the flames, "Blessed Jesus"—
Revealing in two words all sorrows, all hope.
And there is the silence of age,
Too full of wisdom for the tongue to utter it
In words intelligible to those who have not lived
The great range of life.

And there is the silence of the dead.
If we who are in life cannot speak
Of profound experiences,
Why do you marvel that the dead

Do not tell you of death?
Their silence shall be interpreted
As we approach them.

Edgar Lee Masters

THE DARK CAVALIER

I AM the Dark Cavalier; I am the Last Lover:
  My arms shall welcome you when other arms are
      tired;
I stand to wait for you, patient in the darkness,
  Offering forgetfulness of all that you desired.

I ask no merriment, no pretense of gladness,
  I can love heavy lids and lips without their rose;
Though you are sorrowful you will not weary me;
  I will not go from you when all the tired world goes.

I am the Dark Cavalier; I am the Last Lover;
  I promise faithfulness no other lips may keep;
Safe in my bridal place, comforted by darkness,
  You shall lie happily, smiling in your sleep.

Margaret Widdemer

INDIAN SUMMER

(After completing a book for one now dead)

(O Earth-and-Autumn of the Setting Sun,
She is not by, to know my task is done.)
In the brown grasses slanting with the wind,
Lone as a lad whose dog's no longer near,
Lone as a mother whose only child has sinned,
Lone on the loved hill . . . and below me here

The thistle-down in tremulous atmosphere
Along red clusters of the sumach streams;
The shrivelled stalks of golden-rod are sere,
And crisp and white their flashing old racemes.
(. . . forever . . . forever . . . . forever . . .)
This is the lonely season of the year,
This is the season of our lonely dreams.

(*O Earth-and-Autumn of the Setting Sun,*
She is not by, to know my task is done!)
The corn-shocks westward on the stubble plain
Show like an Indian village of dead days;
The long smoke trails behind the crawling train,
And floats atop the distant woods ablaze
With orange, crimson, purple. The low haze
Dims the scarped bluffs above the inland sea,
Whose wide and slaty waters in cold glaze
Await yon full-moon of the night-to-be,
(. . . far . . . and far . . . and far . . .)
These are the solemn horizons of man's ways,
These are the horizons of solemn thought to me.

(*O Earth-and-Autumn of the Setting Sun,*
She is not by, to know my task is done!)
And this the hill she visited, as friend;
And this the hill she lingered on, as bride —
Down in the yellow valley is the end:
They laid her . . . in no evening autumn tide . . .
Under fresh flowers of that May morn, beside
The queens and cave-women of ancient earth . . .

This is the hill . . . and over my city's towers,
Across the world from sunset, yonder in air,

Shines, through its scaffoldings, a civic dome
Of pilèd masonry, which shall be ours
To give, completed, to our children there . . .
And yonder far roof of my abandoned home
Shall house new laughter . . . Yet I tried . . . I tried
And, ever wistful of the doom to come,
I built her many a fire for love . . . for mirth . . .
(When snows were falling on our oaks outside,
Dear, many a winter fire upon the hearth) . . .
(. . . farewell . . . farewell . . . farewell . . .)
We dare not think too long on those who died,
While still so many yet must come to birth.

William Ellery Leonard

DEATH —DIVINATION

DEATH is like moonlight in a lofty wood,
    That pours pale magic through the shadowy leaves;
    'T is like the web that some old perfume weaves
In a dim, lonely room where memories brood;
Like snow-chilled wine it steals into the blood,
    Spurring the pulse its coolness half reprieves;
    Tenderly quickening impulses it gives,
As April winds unsheathe an opening bud.

Death is like all sweet, sense-enfolding things,
    That lift us in a dream-delicious trance
    Beyond the flickering good and ill of chance;
But most is Death like Music's buoyant wings,
    That bear the soul, a willing Ganymede,
    Where joys on joys forevermore succeed.

Charles Wharton Stork

THE MOULD

No doubt this active will,
So bravely steeped in sun,
This will has vanquished Death
And foiled oblivion.

But this indifferent clay,
This fine experienced hand,
So quiet, and these thoughts
That all unfinished stand,

Feel death as though it were
A shadowy caress;
And win and wear a frail
Archaic wistfulness.

Gladys Cromwell

IN PATRIS MEI MEMORIAM

By the fond name that was his own and mine,
    The last upon his lips that strove with doom,
    He called me and I saw the light assume
A sudden glory and around him shine;
And nearer now I saw the laureled line
    Of the august of Song before me loom,
    And knew the voices, erstwhile through the
        gloom,
That whispered and forbade me to repine.
And with farewell, a shaft of splendor sank
    Out of the stars and faded as a flame,

And down the night, on clouds of glory, came
The battle seraphs halting rank on rank;
And lifted heavenward to heroic peace,
He passed and left me hope beyond surcease.
John Myers O'Hara

AD MATREM AMANTISSIMAM ET CARISSIMAM FILII IN ÆTERNUM FIDELITAS

WITH all the fairest angels nearest God,
The ineffable true of heart around the throne,
There shall I find you waiting when the flown
Dream leaves my heart insentient as the clod;
And when the grief-retracing ways I trod
Become a shining path to thee alone,
My weary feet, that seemed to drag as stone,
Shall once again, with wings of fleetness shod,
Fare on, beloved, to find you! Just beyond
The seraph throng await me, standing near
The gentler angels, eager and apart;
Be there, near God's own fairest, with the fond
Sweet smile that was your own, and let me hear
Your voice again and clasp you to my heart.
John Myers O'Hara

AFTERWARDS

THERE was a day when death to me meant tears,
And tearful takings-leave that had to be,
And awed embarkings on an unshored sea,
And sudden disarrangement of the years.
But now I know that nothing interferes

With the fixed forces when a tired man dies;
That death is only answerings and replies,
The chiming of a bell which no one hears,
The casual slanting of a half-spent sun,
The soft recessional of noise and coil,
The coveted something time nor age can spoil;
I know it is a fabric finely spun
Between the stars and dark; to seize and keep,
Such glad romances as we read in sleep.

Mahlon Leonard Fisher

PIERRETTE IN MEMORY

PIERRETTE has gone, but it was not
     Exactly that she died,
So much as vanished and forgot
     To tell where she would hide.

To keep a sudden rendezvous,
     It came into her mind
That she was late. What could she do
     But leave distress behind?

Afraid of being in disgrace,
     And hurrying to dress,
She heard there was another place
     In need of loveliness.

She went so softly and so soon,
     She hardly made a stir;
But going took the stars and moon
     And sun away with her.

William Griffith

THE THREE SISTERS

GONE are the three, those sisters rare
  With wonder-lips and eyes ashine.
One was wise and one was fair,
  And one was mine.

Ye mourners, weave for the sleeping hair
  Of only two, your ivy vine.
For one was wise and one was fair,
  But one was mine.
Arthur Davison Ficke

SONG

. I MAKE my shroud, but no one knows —
So shimmering fine it is and fair,
With stitches set in even rows,
I make my shroud, but no one knows.

In door-way where the lilac blows,
Humming a little wandering air,
I make my shroud and no one knows,
So shimmering fine it is and fair.
Adelaide Crapsey

THE UNKNOWN BELOVÈD

I DREAMED I passed a doorway
  Where, for a sign of death,
White ribbons one was binding
  About a flowery wreath.

What drew me so I know not,
But drawing near I said,
"Kind sir, and can you tell me
Who is it here lies dead?"

Said he, "Your most belovèd
Died here this very day,
That had known twenty Aprils
Had she but lived till May."

Astonished I made answer,
"Good sir, how say you so!
Here have I no belovèd,
This house I do not know."

Quoth he, "Who from the world's end
Was destined unto thee
Here lies, thy true belovèd
Whom thou shalt never see."

I dreamed I passed a doorway
Where, for a sign of death,
White ribbons one was binding
About a flowery wreath.

John Hall Wheelock

CINQUAINS

FATE DEFIED

As it
Were tissue of silver
I'll wear, O fate, thy grey,

And go mistily radiant, clad
Like the moon.

NIGHT WINDS

THE old
Old winds that blew
When chaos was, what do
They tell the clattered trees that I
Should weep?

THE WARNING

JUST now,
Out of the strange
Still dusk . . . as strange, as still . . .
A white moth flew . . . Why am I grown
So cold?

Adelaide Crapsey

THE LONELY DEATH

IN the cold I will rise, I will bathe
In waters of ice; myself
Will shiver, and shrive myself,
Alone in the dawn, and anoint
Forehead and feet and hands;
I will shutter the windows from light,
I will place in their sockets the four
Tall candles and set them aflame
In the grey of the dawn; and myself
Will lay myself straight in my bed,
And draw the sheet under my chin.

Adelaide Crapsey

EXILE FROM GOD

I DO not fear to lay my body down
    In death, to share
The life of the dark earth and lose my own,
    If God is there.

I have so loved all sense of Him, sweet might
    Of color and sound, —
His tangible loveliness and living light
    That robes me 'round.

If to His heart in the hushed grave and dim
    We sink more near,
It shall be well — living we rest in Him.
    Only I fear

Lest from my God in lonely death I lapse,
    And the dumb clod
Lose him; for God is life, and death perhaps
    Exile from God.

           John Hall Wheelock

LOAM

IN the loam we sleep,
In the cool moist loam,
To the lull of years that pass
And the break of stars.

From the loam, then,
The soft warm loam,
    We rise:
To shape of rose leaf,
Of face and shoulder.

We stand, then,
    To a whiff of life,
Lifted to the silver of the sun
Over and out of the loam
    A day.

Carl Sandburg

HILLS OF HOME

NAME me no names for my disease,
    With uninforming breath;
I tell you I am none of these,
    But homesick unto death —

Homesick for hills that I had known,
    For brooks that I had crossed,
Before I met this flesh and bone
    And followed and was lost. . . .

And though they break my heart at last,
    Yet name no name of ills.
Say only, "Here is where he passed,
    Seeking again those hills."

Witter Bynner

THE LAST PIPER

DARK winds of the mountain,
White winds of the sea,
Are skirling the pibroch
Of Seumas an Righ.

The crying of gannets,
The shrieking of terns,
Are keening his dying
High over the burns.

Grey silence of waters
And wasting of lands
And the wailing of music
Down to the sands,

The wailing of music,
And trailing of wind,
The waters before him,
The mountains behind, —

Alone at the gathering,
Silent he stands,
And the wail of his piping
Cries over the lands,

To the moan of the waters,
The drone of the foam,
Where his soul, a white gannet,
Wings silently home.

                    Edward J. O'Brien

THE PROVINCES

O God that I
  May arise with the Gael
To the song in the sky
  Over Inisfail!

Ulster, your dark
  Mold for me;
Munster, a lark
  Hold for me!

Connaght, a *caoine*
  Croon for me;
Lienster, a mean
  Stone for me!

O God that I
  May arise with the Gael
To the song in the sky
  Over Inisfail!

Francis Carlin

OMNIUM EXEUNT IN MYSTERIUM

THE stranger in my gates — lo! that am I,
And what my land of birth I do not know,
Nor yet the hidden land to which I go.
One may be lord of many ere he die,
And tell of many sorrows in one sigh,
But know himself he shall not, nor his woe,
Nor to what sea the tears of wisdom flow;
Nor why one star is taken from the sky.
An urging is upon him evermore,
And though he bide, his soul is wanderer,
Scanning the shadows with a sense of haste —
Where fade the tracks of all who went before:
A dim and solitary traveller
On ways that end in evening and the waste.

George Sterling

MOTH-TERROR

I HAVE killed the moth flying around my night-light;
    wingless and dead it lies upon the floor.
(O who will kill the great Time-Moth that eats holes
    in my soul and that burrows in and through
    my secretest veils!)
My will against its will, and no more will it fly at my
    night-light or be hidden behind the curtains
    that swing in the winds.
(But O who will shatter the Change-Moth that leaves
    me in rags — tattered old tapestries that swing
    in the winds that blow out of Chaos!)
Night-Moth, Change-Moth, Time-Moth, eaters of
    dreams and of me!

Benjamin De Casseres

OLD AGE

I HAVE heard the wild geese,
I have seen the leaves fall,
There was frost last night
On the garden wall.
It is gone to-day
And I hear the wind call.
The wind? . . .That is all.

If the swallow will light
When the evening is near;
If the crane will not scream
Like a soul in fear;

I will think no more
Of the dying year,
And the wind, its seer.

Cale Young Rice

ATROPOS

ATROPOS, dread
  One of the Three,
Holding the thread
  Woven for me;

Grimly thy shears,
  Steely and bright,
Menace the years
  Left for delight.

Grant it may chance,
  Just as they close,
June may entrance
  Earth with the rose;

Reigning as though,
  Bliss to the breath,
Endless and no
  Whisper of death.

John Myers O'Hara

BIOGRAPHICAL NOTES

AIKEN, CONRAD. Born at Savannah, Ga., Aug. 5, 1889. Received the degree of A.B. from Harvard University in 1912 and in August of the same year married Miss Jessie McDonald, of Montreal, Canada. Mr. Aiken's first volume of poetry, "Earth Triumphant," was published in 1914, and has been followed by "Turns and Movies," 1916; "Nocturne of Remembered Spring," 1917; and "The Charnel Rose," 1918. Mr. Aiken is a keen and trenchant critic, as well as a poet, and his volume on the modern movement in poetry, "Skepticisms," is one of the finest and most stimulating contributions to the subject.

AKINS, ZOË. Born at Humansville, Mo., Oct. 30, 1886. Educated at home and at Monticello Seminary, Godfrey, Ill. Miss Akins began her literary work by contributing poems and critical articles to *Reedy's Mirror*, St. Louis, and in 1911 published her volume of poems, "Interpretations." The drama, however, soon began to absorb her, and she has had several plays produced, including "The Magical City," "Papa," a comedy, and "Déclassé," which won a great success with Ethel Barrymore in the leading rôle.

ANDERSON, MARGARET STEELE. Born in Louisville, Ky., and educated in the public schools of that city, with special courses at Wellesley College. Since 1901 Miss Anderson has been Literary Editor of the *Evening Post* of Louisville, and is known as one of the most discriminating critics of the South. She has published but one volume of verse, "The Flame in the Wind," 1914, but it is choice in quality. Miss Anderson is also a critic of Art and is the author of "A Study of Modern Painting."

ARENSBERG, WALTER CONRAD. Mr. Arensberg has been active in the new movement in poetry and was one of the group who contributed to the yearly collection called "Others." He is the author of "Idols," 1916.

BAKER, KARLE WILSON. Born in Little Rock, Ark., Oct. 13, 1878. Educated in public and private schools at Little Rock and at the University of Chicago. Mrs. Baker taught for several years in Virginia and in the High Schools of Little Rock, but in 1901 took up her residence in Texas, whither her family had preceded her, and in 1907 was married to Thomas Ellis Baker, of Nacogdoches, which is her present home. Mrs. Baker is one of the promising new writers, her first volume of verse, "Blue Smoke," having been published in 1919, by the Yale Press.

BATES, KATHARINE LEE. Born at Falmouth, Mass., Aug. 12, 1859. Was educated at Wellesley College, from which she received the degree of A.B., in 1880 and that of A.M. in 1891. She has also had the honorary degree of Litt.D. conferred upon her by Middlebury College and by Oberlin. She has been continuously in educational work, teaching first at Dana Hall and then in Wellesley College, where, since 1891, she has been professor and recently head of the English Department. Miss Bates spent four years in foreign travel and study and has published numerous books in the field of education. Her best-known volumes of verse are: "America the Beautiful," 1911; "Fairy Gold," 1916; and "The Retinue," 1918.

BENÉT, STEPHEN VINCENT. Born at Bethlehem, Pa., 1898. Was educated at the Summerville Academy at Augusta, Ga., and at Yale University, taking the degree of A.B. in 1919 and of A.M. in 1920. His first volume, "Young Adventure," was brought out by the Yale University Press in 1918 and he also contributed largely to the "Yale Book of Student Verse," published in 1919. Mr. Benét is a gifted young writer from whom much may be expected.

BENÉT, WILLIAM ROSE. Born at Fort Hamilton, N.Y. Harbor, Feb. 2, 1886. Graduated at the Academy of Albany, N.Y., in 1904, and took the degree of Ph.B. from the Sheffield Scientific School of Yale University in 1907. In 1912 he was married to Teresa Frances Thompson, of San Francisco, who died in 1919. Mr. Benét was connected for several years with the *Century Magazine*, first as reader and then as assistant editor, a position which he resigned to enter the Aviation Corps of the Army, during the World War. He is now one of the literary editors of the *Evening Post*, of New York. His successive volumes of verse are: "Merchants from Cathay," 1912; "The Falconer of God," 1914; "The Great White Wall," 1916; "The Burglar of the Zodiac," 1918; and "Perpetual Light," 1919.

BRADLEY, WILLIAM ASPINWALL. Born at Hartford, Conn., Feb. 8, 1878. Educated at Columbia University where he received the degree of A.M. in 1900. Married Miss Grace Goodrich in 1903. From 1900 to 1908 Mr. Bradley was art director and literary adviser to McClure, Phillips & Co. and the McClure Co. and left them to become typographical designer and supervisor of printing at the Yale University Press, where he remained until 1917, when America entered the World War. He then became connected with the War Camp Community Service in which he did excellent work for the period of the war. Mr. Bradley is the author of several books and brochures upon art and particularly upon prints and etchings, such as "French Etchers of the Second Empire," 1916. In poetry, he is the author of "Garlands and Wayfarings," 1917; "Old Christmas and Other Kentucky Tales in Verse," 1917; "Singing Carr," 1918. The last two books are based upon Kentucky folk-tales and ballads gathered by Mr. Bradley among the people of the Cumberland Mountains.

BRANCH, ANNA HEMPSTEAD. Born at Hempstead House, New London, Conn. Graduated from Smith College in 1897 and from the American Academy of Dramatic Art, in New York City, in 1900. While at college she began writing poetry and the year after her graduation won the first prize offered by the *Century Magazine* for a poem written by a college graduate. This poem, "The Road 'Twixt Heaven and Hell," was printed in the *Century Magazine* for December, 1898, and was followed soon after by the publication of Miss Branch's first volume, "The Heart of the Road," 1901. She has since published two volumes, "The Shoes That Danced," 1902, and "Rose of the Wind," 1910, both marked by imagination and beauty of a high order.

BURNET, DANA. Born in Cincinnati, Ohio, July 3, 1888. Graduated at the Woodward High School of Cincinnati and took the degree of LL.B. at the Cornell University College of Law in 1911. Married Marguerite E. Dumary, of Brooklyn, in 1913. Mr. Burnet has been associated with the *Evening Sun*, of New York, since 1911, in various capacities, from that of reporter to editor of the magazine page. He is the author of "Poems," 1915, and "The Shining Adventure," 1916.

BURR, AMELIA JOSEPHINE. Educated at Hunter College in the City of New York. Miss Burr has published successively the following books of verse: "A Roadside Fire," 1913; "In Deep Places," 1914; "Life and Living," 1916; "The Silver Trumpet," 1918; and "Hearts Awake," 1919. The last two volumes relate chiefly to the World War.

BURT, MAXWELL STRUTHERS. Born at Baltimore, Md., Oct. 18, 1882. Early education at private schools, Philadelphia. Received the degree of A.B. from Princeton University in 1904 and later studied at Merton College, Oxford University. After two years of teaching at Princeton University, Mr. Burt took up the life of a rancher at Jackson Hole, Wyo., though he usually returns to Princeton for the winter months. In 1913 he married Katharine Newlin, a writer of fiction. Mr. Burt is the author of two volumes of verse, "In the High Hills," 1914, and "Songs and Portraits," 1920; he has also written many short stories.

BYNNER, WITTER. Born at Brooklyn, Aug. 10, 1881. Graduated at Harvard University in 1902. After his graduation, until 1906, he served as assistant editor of *McClure's Magazine* and literary editor of McClure, Phillips & Co. Since that time he has devoted himself exclusively to the writing of poetry and drama, with the exception of a year spent as a special lecturer upon Poetry at the University of California. While at the University, Mr. Bynner's "Canticle of Praise," written to celebrate peace after the World War, was given in the open-air Greek Theatre at Berkeley to an audience of 8000 persons. Mr. Bynner's first volume, "An Ode to Harvard and Other Poems," was published in 1907, and was followed in 1913 by the poetic drama, "Tiger"; in 1915 by "The New World," amplified from his Phi Beta Kappa Poem delivered at Harvard in 1911; in 1917 by "The Little King," a poetic drama; in 1917 also by "Grenstone Poems," a collection of his lyric work to date. In 1916, in connection with his friend, Arthur Davison Ficke, Mr. Bynner perpetrated the clever literary hoax of "Spectra," a volume of verse in the ultra-modern manner, designed to establish a new "school" of poetry that should outdo "Imagism" and other cults then in the public eye. These poems, published under the joint authorship of Emanuel Morgan and Anne Knish, created much comment, and in spite of their bizarre features were taken seriously by well-known critics, who were much discomfited when the truth of the matter was known. In 1919 Mr. Bynner published "The Beloved Stranger," a volume of *vers libre*, written in a style that grew out of the "Spectra" experiment, but divested of its extravagant features.

CARLIN, FRANCIS (JAMES F. C. MacDONNELL). Born April 7, 1881, at Bay Shore, L.I., N.Y. Educated at St. Mary's Parochial School, Norwalk, Conn. Author of "My Ireland," privately printed, 1917 (taken over by Henry Holt & Co. and republished in the following year), "The Cairn of Stars," 1920. Mr. Carlin takes his pen-name from that of his grandfather who was a cottage weaver of linen and a local rhymer in Tyrone, Ireland.

CLEGHORN, SARAH N. Born in Manchester, Vt. Educated at Burr and Burton Seminary, of Manchester. Miss Cleghorn is the author of "Portraits and Protests," 1917.

CONKLING, GRACE HAZARD. Born in New York City. Graduated at Smith College in 1899, and later studied music and languages at the University of Heidelberg and at Paris; was for several years a teacher of English, Latin, and Greek in Woodstock, Conn., and in the schools of New York City. In 1905 she married Roscoe Platt Conkling at San Antonio, Texas, and spent her early married life in Mexico, which inspired some of her most charming lyrics. Since 1914, Mrs.

Conkling has been teaching in the English Department of Smith College. She has published "Afternoons in April," 1915, and "Wilderness Songs," 1920. Mrs. Conkling is a poet of exceedingly delicate and beautiful touch, and her gift seems to have been transmitted to her daughter, Hilda, whose poems written, or told, between the ages of five and eight, and published in a volume in 1920, prove her to be a child of remarkable poetic talent.

CORBIN, ALICE (MRS. WM. PENHALLOW HENDERSON). Born in St. Louis, of Southern parentage. Educated at the University of Chicago. Since its founding in 1912, Mrs. Henderson has been associate editor, with Harriet Monroe, of *Poetry, A Magazine of Verse,* and also co-editor, with Miss Monroe, of "The New Poetry," an anthology of modern English and American poets. She is the author of "Adam's Dream and Two Other Miracle Plays for Children" (in verse), and of a collection of poems called "The Spinning Woman of the Sky."

COX, ELEANOR ROGERS. Born at Enniskillen, Ireland. Came with family to the United States in childhood; citizen; educated at St. Gabriel's High School and private tuition. Although Miss Cox has lived in America since childhood, her poetic inspiration has come chiefly from the myths and legends of Ireland, her mother country, to which she returns at intervals. Her two volumes of verse, "A Hosting of Heroes," 1911, and "Singing Fires of Erin," 1916, are instinct with the Celtic spirit. Miss Cox also lectures upon Irish legendry.

CRAPSEY, ADELAIDE. Born in Brooklyn, Sept. 9, 1878. Her young girlhood was spent in Rochester, N.Y., where her father, Algernon S. Crapsey, was rector of St. Andrew's Episcopal Church. After preparatory work in Kemper Hall, Kenosha, Wis., she entered Vassar College, graduating, as a Phi Beta Kappa, in 1901. After two years of teaching at Kemper Hall, Miss Crapsey went to Italy and became a student at the School of Archæology in Rome, at the same time giving lectures in Italian history. Upon returning to America she taught history and literature for two years in a private school at Stamford, Conn., but gave up her work because of ill health and spent the following two years in Italy and England, working upon her "Study of English Metrics." Recovering sufficiently to do so, she returned to this country in 1911 and took a position as Instructor of Poetics at Smith College, but in 1913 was obliged to resign because of renewed illness and died on the 8th of October, 1914. After her death, the Manas Press of Rochester brought out a small volume of her poetry, and her "Study of English Metrics" was published in 1918 by Alfred Knopf. Adelaide

Crapsey had a rarely beautiful and original poetic gift, and her early death is greatly to be regretted.

CROMWELL, GLADYS. Born in Brooklyn, but lived the greater part of her life in New York City. She was educated at private schools in New York, and had a period of study in Paris, supplemented by extensive foreign travel. At the outbreak of the World War, Miss Cromwell and her twin sister volunteered for service in the Red Cross and were actively engaged both in canteen work and in hospital service. The strain proved too great and induced a mental depression, which, acting upon the highly sensitive nature of the sisters, caused them to feel that they had no longer a place in a world which held no refuge for beauty and quiet thought, and on their way home from France, in January of 1919, they committed suicide by jumping from the deck of the steamer Loraine. Three months later they were buried in France with military honors and the French Government awarded them the Croix de Guerre and the Médaille de Reconnaissance française. The poetry of Gladys Cromwell is deeply thoughtful and almost sculptural in its chiseled beauty. It shows the reaction of a finely tempered spirit to a world at variance with it. Had Miss Cromwell lived she would almost certainly have added some distinguished work to our poetry, since the lyrics contained in the volume of her verse issued after her death are of so fine a quality.

DARGAN, OLIVE TILFORD. Born in Grayson County, Ky., and educated at the University of Nashville and at Radcliffe College. She became a teacher and was connected with various schools in Arkansas, Missouri, and Texas until her marriage. Mrs. Dargan's first work was in poetic drama in which she revealed gifts of a high order. Her dramatic volumes are: "Semiramis, and Other Plays," 1904; "Lords and Lovers," 1906, and "The Mortal Gods," 1912. As a lyric poet Mrs. Dargan has done some beautiful work, most of which may be found in her collection "Path Flower," 1914, and she has also published a sequence of fine sonnets under the title of "The Cycle's Rim," 1916.

DAVIES, MARY CAROLYN (MRS. LELAND DAVIS). Miss Davies was born and educated in California and came to New York from her home in that state, where she soon began to attract attention by the fresh and original quality of her verse, which appeared frequently in the magazines. In 1918 she married Leland Davis. In the same year she published "The Drums in Our Street," a book of war verse, and in 1919 brought out a much finer and more characteristic collection of her poems under the title, "Youth Riding." Miss Davies has also written several one-act plays, one of which, "The Slave with Two Faces," has had successful presentation.

DAVIS, FANNIE STEARNS (MRS. AUGUSTUS MCKINSTREY GIFFORD). Born at Cleveland, Ohio, March 6, 1884. Educated at Smith College, from which she graduated in 1904. She is the author of two volumes of poetry: "Myself and I," 1913, and "Crack o' Dawn," 1915, both marked by unusually sensitive feeling and delicate artistry.

DE CASSERAS, BENJAMIN. Born in Philadelphia in 1873, of old Spanish and American stock and educated in the public schools of Philadelphia. He entered the office of the *Philadelphia Press* in 1889 and served for ten years on the paper in every capacity from that of proof-reader to theatrical critic and editorial writer. In 1899 he came to New York and entered the newspaper field, working successively on the *Sun*, the *Herald*, and the *Times*. For a short time he was engaged in journalistic work in Mexico, having been cofounder, in 1906, of *El Diario* in the City of Mexico. Since that time he has been a voluminous contributor to magazines and has published books in many fields, since he is poet, essayist, critic, and satirist. As a poet his best-known work is in "The Shadow-Eater," 1915. Among his other volumes are "The Chameleon," "Forty Immortals," "Edelweiss and Mandragora," and "Counsels of Imperfection," translated into French by Remy de Gourmont.

DRISCOLL, LOUISE. Born in Poughkeepsie, educated by private teachers and in the public schools of Catskill, N.Y. Miss Driscoll first attracted attention by a poem called "Metal Checks" which received a prize of $100 offered by *Poetry: A Magazine of Verse*, for the best poem on the European war. Since then Miss Driscoll has been a constant contributor to the best magazines, but has not yet published a collection of her verse.

FICKE, ARTHUR DAVISON. Born Davenport, Iowa, Nov. 10, 1883. Educated at Harvard University where he graduated in 1904. Later he studied at the College of Law of the Iowa State University and was admitted to the bar in 1903. In 1907 he married Evelyn Bethune Blunt, of Springfield, Mass. Mr. Ficke has published many books of verse of which the best-known are "The Earth Passion," 1908; "Sonnets of a Portrait Painter," 1914; "The Man on the Hilltop," 1915; "An April Elegy," 1917. Mr. Ficke has also written two volumes upon "Japanese Painting" and "Japanese Prints," in part the outcome of a trip to Japan, taken in company with his friend Witter Bynner. As mentioned in the sketch of Mr. Bynner, Mr. Ficke was associated with him in writing the volume, "Spectra."

FISHER, MAHLON LEONARD. Born in Williamsport, Pa., July 20, 1874. Educated in private study and in the schools of his native city. Mr. Fisher took up architecture and practiced this profession for seventeen years, but although he still retains connection with it in a consulting capacity, he has given up its active practice to be the publisher and editor of a small magazine called *The Sonnet*, which he founded. Mr. Fisher has written some of the finest sonnets that have appeared in America in recent years and has brought out the first collection of them under the title, "Sonnets: A First Series," 1918.

FLETCHER, JOHN GOULD. Born at Little Rock, Ark., Jan. 3, 1886. He was educated in the public schools of Little Rock, in Phillips Academy, Andover, and at Harvard University, but becoming restive under the formal curriculum did not stay to take his degree, but went instead to Europe where he might find an atmosphere more in harmony with his tastes and interests. Italy first attracted him and he remained there for several years, but went in May of 1909 to London where he has spent most of the time since that date. In 1913 he published five small books of verse, all of which are now out of print, but it was not until the publication of "Irradiations — Sand and Spray" in America in 1915 that his true poetic quality was evident. In the same year several poems of his appeared in "Some Imagist Poets," the first joint collection of the Imagist group, which embraced the work of Amy Lowell, Richard Aldington, "H. D.", F. S. Flint, D. H. Lawrence, and Mr. Fletcher himself. This allied him with the Imagist movement, though his work was too individual to conform to any school. The war drove Mr. Fletcher back to America where he remained two years, and in April of 1916 he published in this country "Goblins and Pagodas"; the following month he returned to England and married Miss Florence Emily Arbuthnot. He continues to make England his home and brought out there his latest volume, "The Tree of Life."

FOSTER, JEANNE ROBERT. Born in the Adirondack Mountains in the town of Johnsburg, N.Y., of English and French stock. Attended the schools of the neighborhood and at the age of sixteen began teaching. Two years later she came to New York, studied at the Stanhope-Wheatcroft Dramatic School, and played upon the stage for one year. Not satisfied with this life, however, she went to Boston, took special courses in the Radcliffe-Harvard Extension and at Boston University, and began writing for the press. Married Matlock Foster and came to New York in 1911 where she became associated with the *Review of Reviews* as literary editor, hold ing this position until 1919. Mrs. Foster has published two books of verse, "Wild Apples" and "Neighbors of Yesterday," both 1916. In the latter she writes, with much narrative skill, of the isolated mountain folk whom she knew in her girlhood.

FROST, ROBERT. Born in San Francisco, March 26, 1875. Studied at Dartmouth College and Harvard University from 1892 to 1899. Married Miss Elinor M. White, of Lawrence, Mass., and went to live upon a farm at Derry, N.H., where he followed the occupation of farming from 1900 to 1905. Finding it, however, scarcely adequate to the needs of his family, he began teaching English at the Pinkerton Academy at Derry and held this position until 1911 when he became a teacher of psychology in the State Normal School at Plymouth, N.H. In 1912 he took perhaps the most important step in his life up to that period, and with his wife and four young children went to England where he might find a more sympathetic atmosphere for creative work. Most of the poems in "A Boy's Will," his earliest collection, were written prior to his residence in England, but few had been published, and the book was not finally issued in America until after the appearance of "North of Boston," the volume upon which his recognition was based. This book, published first in England, and reprinted in America in 1914, was received with enthusiasm by the foremost English critics who recognized in it a note distinctively individual and distinctively American, and Mr. Frost came back to this country after three years of delightful and fruitful life in England, where he had enjoyed the close companionship of Masefield, Gibson, Abercrombie, and others of the English group — to find his work widely known and appreciated. Nothing finer nor more significant has come out of our poetic revival than Mr. Frost's work, which reflects the life of New England in its more isolated aspects, and interprets the spirit of the people with the keenest insight and the most sympathetic understanding. In the way of form, Mr. Frost has also been a path-finder, building his poems primarily upon the rhythms of the speaking voice. "North of Boston" was followed in 1916 by "A Mountain Interval," containing some beautiful lyric as well as narrative work.

GARRISON, THEODOSIA (MRS. FREDERICK J. FAULKS). Born at Newark, N.J. Educated at private schools in New York. Mrs. Garrison was for several years a constant contributor to the magazines, but has written less of late. Her volumes of verse are: "Joy o' Life," 1908, "The Earth Cry," 1910, and "The Dreamers," 1917.

GILTINAN, CAROLINE. Born in Philadelphia, Pa. Educated

in the public schools of that city and at the University of Pennsylvania. Miss Giltinan served very conspicuously abroad during the World War, as an army nurse, and later in an important position in the Department of Sick and Wounded. She is the author of "The Divine Image," 1917.

GRIFFITH, WILLIAM. Born Memphis, Mo., Feb. 15, 1876. Educated in public schools. Married Florence Vernon, of Brooklyn, in 1909. Mr. Griffith has had an active career in the newspaper profession, having been on the staff of several of the New York papers, managing editor of *Hampton's Magazine*, 1906–10; editor, *McCall's Magazine*, 1911–12; editorial director of the *National Sunday Magazine*, a large newspaper syndicate, 1912–16; since then associate editor of *Current Opinion*. His best-known books of verse are: "City Views and Visions," 1911; "Loves and Losses of Pierrot," 1916; "City Pastorals," 1918; "The House of the Sphinx and Other Poems," 1918.

GUITERMAN, ARTHUR. Born, of American parentage, at Vienna, Austria, Nov. 20, 1871. Graduated at the College of the City of New York in 1891. Married Vida Lindo, of New York, 1909. Mr. Guiterman did editorial work on the *Woman's Home Companion* and the *Literary Digest* from 1891 to 1906, and published several books of verse, now out of print, before doing those which contain his representative work: "The Laughing Muse," 1915; "The Mirthful Lyre," 1917; and "Ballads of Old New York," 1920. While Mr. Guiterman is widely known as a humorous poet, he is also an accomplished poet in other moods.

"H. D." (HELENA DOOLITTLE). Born at Bethlehem, Pa., Sept. 10, 1886. Educated at the Gordon School and the Friends' Central School of Philadelphia and at Bryn Mawr College. Miss Doolittle went to Europe in 1911 and, after a tour of the Continent, settled down in London, where she was soon caught into the current of the poetic movement then shaping itself under the innovating genius of Ezra Pound and a little band of his fellow poets. Under this stimulus Miss Doolittle began to write those brief, sharply carved poems, purely Greek in their chastity and mood, of which the first group appeared in *Poetry* for Jan., 1913, under the name of "H. D. — Imagist." Among the London poets interested in experiments with new forms was Richard Aldington, whose own inspiration came largely from the Greek, and in October of 1913 he and Miss Doolittle were married and the work of both appeared in the little volume, "Des Imagistes," published in New York in April, 1914. This was the first grouping of the Imagist school, whose work, without that of Ezra

Pound, its founder, who withdrew from the movement, continued for several years to appear in America under the title of "Some Imagist Poets." Since then one volume of "H. D.'s." own work has been published, "Sea Garden," London and Boston, 1917. For the finest and most comprehensive study of "H. D.'s" work see "Tendencies in Modern American Poetry," by Amy Lowell, 1917.

HAGEDORN, HERMANN. Born in New York City, July 18, 1882. Educated at Harvard University and University of Berlin. Served as Instructor at Harvard from 1909 to 1911. Married Dorothy Oakley of Englewood, N.J., 1908. Mr. Hagedorn is the author of "The Silver Blade, a Play in Verse," 1907; "The Woman of Corinth," 1908; "A Troop of the Guard," 1909; "Poems and Ballads," 1911; "The Great Maze and the Heart of Youth," 1916; and "Hymn of Free Peoples Triumphant," 1918. Mr. Hagedorn is an ardent American and organized "The Vigilantes," a body of writers to do patriotic work with the pen during the World War. Edited "Fifes and Drums," a collection of war poetry, 1917.

HARDING, RUTH GUTHRIE. Born at Tunkhannock, Pa., Aug. 20, 1882. Educated at Wyoming Seminary, Kingston, Pa., and at Bucknell University. Married John Ward Harding of Pateson, N.J., Oct. 1901. Mrs. Harding is the author of "A Lark Went Singing," 1916.

HOYT, HELEN. Born at Norwalk, Conn. Educated at Barnard College. Has been connected with *Poetry*, of Chicago, as associate editor. Miss Hoyt has contributed to the best magazines for several years, but has not, as yet, published a volume of verse.

JOHNS, ORRICK. Born in St. Louis, Mo., in 1887. Educated at the University of Missouri and at Washington University in St. Louis. Was associated for a short time with *Reedy's Mirror*. In 1912 he received the first prize, of $500, for a poem entitled "Second Avenue," contributed to the contest of "The Lyric Year" and afterwards published in that volume. Since then Mr. Johns has written "Asphalt," 1917, which contains his charming group of poems, "Country Rhymes," the best of his lyric work.

JONES, THOMAS S., JR. Born at Boonville, N.Y., Nov. 6 1882. Graduated at Cornell University in 1904. He was on the dramatic staff of the *New York Times* from 1904 to 1907, and associate editor of *The Pathfinder* in 1911. His published volumes are: "Path of Dreams," 1904; "From Quiet Valleys," 1907; "Interludes," 1908; "Ave Atque Vale" (In Memoriam Arthur Upson), 1909; "The Voice in the Silence," with a Foreword by James Lane Allen, 1911; and "The Rose-Jar," originally published in 1906, but taken over in 1915 by

Thomas B. Mosher and made the initial volume of "Lyra Americana," his first series of American poetry. Mr. Mosher has also added "The Voice in the Silence" to this series. Mr. Jones is a poet of rare delicacy and fineness whose work has gathered to itself a discriminating group of readers.

KEMP, HARRY. Born in Youngstown, Ohio, Dec. 15, 1883, but came East in his childhood. Mr. Kemp has had a most romantic and picturesque career. He ran away from High School to go to sea, shipping first to Australia. From there he went to China, and eventually returned to America *via* California. Coming East again, he prepared for college at Mt. Hermon school, N.J., and entered the University of Kansas, where he remained until his graduation in his twenty-sixth year. Since then, with the exception of a winter in London, he has lived in New York, where he is associated with the Greenwich Village group of dramatic folk, both playwrights and actors. Mr. Kemp has written many brief dramas and produced them with his own company at a small theater in New York, but it is in poetry that he has done his best work thus far. He has the true lyric quality, as shown in his two volumes, "Poems," and "The Passing God," 1919.

KILMER, ALINE (MRS. JOYCE KILMER). Born Norfolk, Va. Daughter of the poet Ada Foster Murray. Educated in public schools and at the Vail-Deane School of Elizabeth, N.J. Married in 1908 to Joyce Kilmer, who met death in France during the World War. Mrs. Kilmer is the author of "Candles that Burn," 1919, which contains some of the sincerest and most moving lyric poetry that has come out of our present revival.

KILMER, JOYCE. Born at New Brunswick, N.J., Dec. 6, 1886. Educated at Columbia University. After a short period of teaching he became associated with the Funk and Wagnalls Company, where he remained from 1909 to 1912 when he assumed the position of literary editor of *The Churchman*. His next step was to associate himself with the staff of the *New York Times*, where he became a well-known feature writer, doing in particular a series of interviews with literary people which were later incorporated into a book. During this period he contributed poetry to the leading magazines and published several collections, of which the first, "A Summer of Love," was published in 1911 and was followed by "Trees, and Other Poems," 1914, and "Main Street and Other Poems," 1917. His work, human in mood, mellow in quality, full of tenderness and reverence for the old sanctities, soon drew to itself a large audience, an audience greatly enhanced by the poet's personal contacts. His kindly and whimsical humor, his charm of personality, his enthusiasm and sympathy, won for him a large group of friends and radiated to the wider group who became his readers. In 1908 he married Aline Murray, herself a poet, and several children were born to them, celebrated in the poems of both parents. Upon America's entry into the World War, Joyce Kilmer enlisted, and after a short period of training was sent to France with the 165th Infantry, formerly the "Fighting 69th," a regiment of Irish blood and of the Catholic religion, to which he had himself become an adherent. He was made a sergeant and served with conspicuous gallantry, so much so, indeed, that it was said of him by the chaplain of the regiment that he "had a romantic passion for death in battle." He was promoted to the Intelligence Department of the service where the personal risk was the greatest, and was killed in action at the battle of the Ourcq, July 30, 1918. He was buried within sound of the river. Since his death two volumes containing his complete work in prose and verse, his letters from abroad, and an excellent memoir written by his friend, Robert Holliday, have been published and will do much to perpetuate the memory of this beloved soldier-poet.

KREYMBORG, ALFRED. Born in New York City and educated in the public schools of New York. Mr. Kreymborg was the founder and editor of a little magazine called *Others,* which became the organ of a group of insurgent poets. Also under the title of "Others," he has issued at intervals selections from the work of these poets, forming a novel and interesting anthology. In addition to writing poetry which he has published in a collection called "Mushrooms," 1917, Mr. Kreymborg is the author of several brief poetic plays which he presents as "Poem-Mimes," performed by puppets.

LEE, AGNES (MRS. OTTO FREER). Born in Chicago, Ill. Educated in Switzerland. Married, 2d, Otto Freer, 1911. Author of "The Round Rabbit," 1898; "The Border of the Lake," 1910; "The Sharing," 1914; translator of the poems of Théophile Gautier, and of "The Gates of Childhood," by Fernand Gregh. A contributor of poems to the leading magazines, particularly *Poetry,* of Chicago.

LEE, MUNA. Miss Lee spent her early life in Oklahoma, and first came into notice as a poet by gaining a prize given by *Poetry,* of Chicago, for the best lyric verse by a young writer. She afterward came to New York and married Luis Marin, of South America. Is at present living in Porto Rico; has not, as yet, published a volume of poetry.

LEDOUX, LOUIS V. Born in New York City, June 6, 1880. Educated at Columbia University where he graduated in 1902. He is a poet who writes chiefly upon Greek themes

and is the author of "Songs from the Silent Land," 1905;
"The Soul's Progress," 1907; "Yzdra: A Poetic Drama,"
1909; "The Shadow of Ætna," 1914; "The Story of Eleusis:
A Lyrical Drama," 1916.

LEONARD, WILLIAM ELLERY. Born at Plainfield, N.J., Jan.
25, 1876. A.B. Boston University, 1898; A.M. Harvard, 1899.
Fellow of Boston University in philology and literature, 1900;
student University of Göttingen, 1901; University of Bonn,
1902; fellow of Columbia University, 1902–03; Ph.D. Columbia, 1904. After receiving these various degrees, Mr. Leonard
began his work as Instructor of Latin at Boston University,
going from there to the University of Wisconsin where he has
remained continuously since 1906, as Assistant Professor of
English. He has written extensively on classic subjects, in
addition to his work in poetry, and has also published volumes in the field of literary criticism. His best-known works
are: "Byron and Byronism in America," 1905; "Sonnets and
Poems," 1906; "The Fragments of Empedocles," 1908; "The
Poet of Galilee," 1909; "The Vaunt of Man," 1912; "Glory
of the Morning," a play, 1912; "Æsop and Hyssop," 1913.
Mr. Leonard has also made a remarkable blank-verse translation of Lucretius, which was published in 1916, and has
translated from the Greek and the German.

LINDSAY, VACHEL. Born in Springfield, Ill., Nov. 10, 1879.
Educated at Hiram College, Ohio. His first intention was to
enter the field of art and he became a student at the Art Institute of Chicago where he remained from 1900 to 1903, con-
tinuing his work at the New York School of Art, 1904–05,
under the personal instruction of Wm. Chase and Robert
Henri. For a time after his technical study, he lectured upon
art in its practical relation to the community, and returning
to his home in Springfield, Ill., issued what might be termed
his manifesto in the shape of "The Village Magazine," divided
about equally between prose articles pertaining to the beauti-
fying of his native city, and poems, illustrated by his own
drawings. Both the verse and drawings showed a delightful
imagination; the poetry in particular, unlike the more elabo-
rate technique of his later work, had a Blake-like simplicity.
Soon after the publication of "The Village Magazine," Mr.
Lindsay, taking as scrip for the journey, "Rhymes to be
Traded for Bread," made a pilgrimage on foot through several Western States, going as far afield as New Mexico. The
story of this journey is given in his volume, "Adventures
While Preaching the Gospel of Beauty," 1916. Mr. Lindsay
had taken an earlier journey on foot, from Jacksonville, Fla.,
to Springfield, Ill., which he has recorded in "A Handy Guide
for Beggars," also 1916. This is much the finer volume of the

two and should take its place with the permanent literature of vagabondage. In 1913 Mr. Lindsay came into wide notice by his poem, "General William Booth Enters into Heaven," which became the title poem of his first volume of verse, published in 1913. This was followed by "The Congo," 1914; "The Chinese Nightingale," 1917, and "Golden Whales of California," 1920. Mr. Lindsay has based all of his later work upon the idea of poetry as a spoken art and has developed it particularly along the line of rhythm. His work is unique, he adheres to no "school," nor has he found imitators. He renders his own work so as to bring out all of its rhythmic possibilities and has become quite as well known for his interpretations of his work as for the work itself. Much of his verse is social in appeal, but he is at his best in poems of more imaginative beauty, such as "The Chinese Nightingale."

LOWELL, AMY. Born in Brookline, Mass., Feb. 9, 1874. Educated at private schools. Author of "A Dome of Many-Colored Glass," 1912; "Sword Blades and Poppy Seed," 1914; "Men, Women and Ghosts," 1916; "Can Grande's Castle," 1918; "Pictures of the Floating World," 1919. Editor of the three successive collections of "Some Imagist Poets," 1915, '16, and '17, containing the early work of the "Imagist School" of which Miss Lowell became the leader. This movement, of which we have spoken in the notes upon the work of "H. D." and John Gould Fletcher, originated in England, the idea having been first conceived by a young poet named T. E. Hulme, but developed and put forth by Ezra Pound in an article called "Don'ts by an Imagist," which appeared in *Poetry; A Magazine of Verse*. As previously stated, a small group of poets gathered about Mr. Pound, experimenting along the technical lines suggested, and a cult of "Imagism" was formed, whose first group-expression was in the little volume, "Des Imagistes," published in New York in April, 1914. Miss Lowell did not come actively into the movement until after that time, but once she had entered it, she became its leader, and it was chiefly through her effort in America that the movement attained so much prominence and so influenced the trend of poetry for the years immediately succeeding. Miss Lowell has many times, in admirable articles, stated the principles upon which Imagism is based, notably in the Preface to "Some Imagist Poets" and in the Preface to the second series, in 1916. She has also elaborated it much more fully in her volume, "Tendencies in Modern American Poetry," 1917, in the articles pertaining to the work of "H. D." and John Gould Fletcher. In her own creative work, however, Miss Lowell has done most to establish the possibilities of the Imagistic idea and of its modes of presentation, and has opened up many interesting avenues of poetic form. Her volume, "Can Grande's Castle," is devoted to work in the medium which she has styled "Polyphonic Prose" and contains some of her finest work, particularly "The Bronze Horses."

MASTERS, EDGAR LEE. Born Garnett, Kan., Aug. 23, 1869. Educated at Knox College, Ill. He studied law in his father's office and was admitted to the bar in 1891. Married Helen M. Jenkins, of Chicago, in 1898. Mr. Masters wrote several volumes of verse and several poetic dramas, which are now out of print, before he found himself in the "Spoon River Anthology," published first in *Reedy's Mirror* and in book form in 1915. This volume, written in free verse and containing about two hundred brief sketches, or posthumous confessions, shows Mr. Masters to be a psychologist of the keenest penetration, a satirist and humorist, laying bare unsparingly the springs of human weakness, but seeing with an equal insight humanity's finer side. "Spoon River Anthology," which had perhaps a wider recognition than that of any volume of verse of the period, was followed by "Songs and Satires," 1916; "The Great Valley," 1916; "Toward the Gulf," 1917; and "Starved Rock," 1920.

MIDDLETON, SCUDDER. Born in New York City, Sept. 9, 1888. Educated at Columbia University. Was connected for several years with the publishing firm of The Macmillan Company. Mr. Middleton is the author of "Streets and Faces," 1917, and "The New Day," 1919.

MILLAY, EDNA ST. VINCENT. Born at Camden, Maine, and educated at Vassar College. Before entering college, however, when she was but nineteen years of age, she wrote the poem, "Renascence," entered in the prize contest of "The Lyric Year," a poem showing a remarkable imagination in so young a writer. After leaving college Miss Millay came to New York and became associated with the Provincetown Players for whom she wrote several one-act plays in which she herself acted the leading part. Her plays have also been produced by other companies and have attracted the attention of critics, particularly the poetic drama, "Aria da Capo," 1920. Miss Millay is one of our most gifted young poets. Her volumes of verse to date are: "Renascence, and Other Poems," 1917, and "Poems," 1920.

MONROE, HARRIET. Born in Chicago. Graduated at Visitation Academy, Georgetown, D.C., March, 1891. Miss Monroe was chosen to write the ode for the dedication of the World's Columbian Exposition in Chicago in 1892. After some years in literary work, chiefly as an art critic, Miss Monroe founded, in October of 1912, *Poetry; A Magazine of*

Verse, an organ which has done much to stimulate interest in poetry and also its production, since it has become the recognized vehicle for the work of the newer school. The first "Imagist" poems appeared in its pages and it was the first to print the work of Carl Sandburg and other well-known poets of the poetic revival. Miss Monroe is the author of "Valeria and Other Poems," 1892; "The Passing Show, Modern Plays in Verse," 1903; "You and I," 1914, and was co-editor, with Alice Corbin Henderson, of "The New Poetry," an anthology, 1917.

MORGAN, ANGELA. Born in Washington, D.C. Educated by private tutors, the public schools, and by special University courses. Miss Morgan entered the journalistic field while still a young girl and did very brilliant work on papers of Chicago and New York. Her work covered all phases of life from those of society to the slums. She visited police courts, jails, and all places where humanity suffers and struggles, and it was no doubt her early work in the newspaper field that gave to her later work, both in poetry and fiction, its strong social bias. Probably no poet of the present time responds more keenly to the social needs of the period, nor has a keener sense of the opportunity for service. Miss Morgan was one of the delegates to the First International Congress of Women, at The Hague, during the first year of the war, and has appeared frequently in readings from her own work. Her volumes of verse are "The Hour Has Struck," 1914; "Utterance and Other Poems," 1916; "Forward, March," 1918; and "Hail, Man," 1919. She has also published a volume of stories under the title "The Imprisoned Splendor."

MORTON, DAVID. Born in Elkton, Ky., Feb. 21, 1886. Educated in the public schools of Louisville, Ky., and at Vanderbilt University, Nashville, Tenn., where he graduated with the degree of B.S. in 1909. Mr. Morton first took up journalism and was reporter and associate editor of various Southern periodicals up to 1915, when he entered the teaching profession as Professor of English at the Boys' High School of Louisville. He is now teacher of History and English at the Morristown High School, Morristown, N.J. In 1919 Mr. Morton took the first prize, of $150, for the best poem read at the Poetry Society of America during the current year, and in 1920 he was awarded a $500 prize for one of three book manuscripts considered the best submitted to the contest of "The Lyric Society." The volume, "Ships in Harbor, and Other Poems," will be published in the autumn of 1920. Mr. Morton is one of the finest sonneteers of this period and a poet of rare and authentic gifts.

NEIHARDT, JOHN G. Born at Sharpsburg, Ill., Jan. 8, 1881. Removed in his early boyhood to Bancroft, Neb., his present home. He has made a special study of the pioneer life of the West and also of the Indian life, having spent some time among the Omaha Indians. His work has great virility and sweep and he has a fine gift of narrative. His first volume, "A Bundle of Myrrh," 1908, showed unmistakably that a new poet had appeared in the West. This was followed by the lyric collections, "Man-Song," 1909; "The Stranger at the Gate," 1912; and "The Quest," 1916. Mr. Neihardt then turned his attention to the writing of a trilogy of narrative poems, each devoted to some character identified with the pioneer life of the Far West. "The Song of Hugh Glass," 1915, and "The Song of Three Friends," 1919, have thus far been published. The material used by Mr. Neihardt is not only romantic and picturesque, but valuable in the historical sense and he is able to shape it with dramatic imagination.

NORTON, GRACE FALLOW. Born at Northfield, Minn., Oct. 29, 1876. Author of "Little Gray Songs from St. Joseph's," 1912; "The Sister of the Wind," 1914; "Roads," 1915; and "What is Your Legion?" 1916.

O'BRIEN, EDWARD JOSEPH. Born in Boston, Mass., Dec. 10, 1890. Educated at Boston College and Harvard University. Author of "White Fountains," 1917; "The Forgotten Threshold," 1918. Editor of "The Masque of Poets," 1918. Since 1915 Mr. O'Brien has been editing a collection of "The Best Short Stories" of the current season.

O'CONOR, NORREYS JEPHSON. Born in New York City, Dec. 31, 1885. Was educated at Harvard University where he took the degrees of A.B. and A.M., making a special study of the Gaelic language and literature in which he has also done some valuable research work. Having, through his own Celtic descent, a particular interest in Ireland and its literature, and having spent a part of his time in that country, Mr. O'Conor's poetry naturally turns upon Celtic themes which have inspired some excellent dramatic as well as lyric work from his pen. His volumes in their order are: "Celtic Memories," 1914; "Beside the Blackwater," 1915; "The Fairy Bride: A Play in Three Acts," 1916; and "Songs of the Celtic Past," 1918.

O'HARA, JOHN MYERS. Born at Cedar Rapids, Iowa. Educated at Northwestern University, Evanston, Ill. Was admitted to the bar and practiced law in Chicago for twelve years, when he gave up this profession and came to New York to become a stock-broker. Although Mr. O'Hara has followed this exacting occupation for the past ten years, it has not prevented him from writing and publishing several volumes of poetry, largely classic in theme, and handled with an adequate and beautiful art. "The Poems of Sappho," 1907, built upon the authentic fragments, are acknowledged to be among the finest in English literature. Mr. O'Hara's other volumes comprise: "Songs of the Open," 1909; "Pagan Sonnets," 1910; "The Ebon Muse," 1912; "Manhattan," 1915; and "Threnodies," 1918.

O SHEEL, SHAEMAS. Born in New York City, Sept. 19, 1886. Educated at Columbia University. His two volumes of verse are: "The Blossomy Bough," 1911, and "The Light Feet of Goats," 1915. Mr. O Sheel is a true poet, writing in the Celtic tradition.

OPPENHEIM, JAMES. Born at St. Paul, Minn., May 24, 1882, but a resident of New York City, where he has spent most of his life. He was educated at Columbia University and first entered sociological work, becoming assistant head worker at the Hudson Guild Settlement, 1901–03. Married Lucy Seckel, of New York, June, 1905. Was teacher and acting superintendent of the Hebrew Technical School for Girls, New York, 1905–07, when he left to engage entirely in literary work. Mr. Oppenheim is a well-known short-story writer and novelist as well as poet, but we will confine ourselves to listing his work in poetry, which has in itself been voluminous. Since his first collection, "Monday Morning and Other Poems," 1909, his work has been written chiefly in free verse, or in "polyphonic poetry," to use his own term, usually in sweeping rhythms more akin to those of Whitman than to the later free-verse writers. In spirit, too, he has the Whitman mood, or rather, he is absorbed by the same great social and democratic aspects of life. Few poets see life so broadly as Mr. Oppenheim or look as deeply below its surface; his work, however, is beset technically by the danger that attends a poet who works in a semi-prose medium, and the art is not always commensurate with the thought. Mr. Oppenheim's other volumes of verse are: "Pioneers," a poetic play, 1910; "Songs for the New Age," 1914; "War and Laughter," 1916; "The Book of Self," 1917; "The Solitary," 1919.

PEABODY, JOSEPHINE PRESTON (MRS. LIONEL MARKS). Born in New York City. Educated at the Girls' Latin School of Boston and at Radcliffe College. Miss Peabody was Instructor of English at Wellesley College from 1901 to 1903. Her volumes in their order are: "The Wayfarers," 1898; "Fortune and Men's Eyes," 1900; "Marlowe, a Drama," 1901; "The Singing Leaves," 1903; "The Wings," 1905; "The Piper," a drama, awarded the Stratford-on-Avon Prize of $1500 in 1910; "The Singing Man," 1911; "The Wolf of Gubbio," a drama, 1913; and "The Harvest Moon," 1916. Miss Peabody's charming play, "The Piper," first produced at Stratford, was played also in New York at the Century Theater, having a successful run, and was revived in the winter of 1920 by the Drama League. Miss Peabody is a poet of a very delicate and individual art, whether in lyric or drama.

PERCY, WILLIAM ALEXANDER. Born in Greenville, Miss., May 14, 1885. Was prepared for college chiefly by a Roman Catholic priest; went to the University of the South, at Sewanee, Tenn., where he received his B.A. degree. The next year he spent abroad, and the following entered Harvard Law School, where he took the degree of LL.B. He is now in the active practice of law in Greenville, Miss. His first book of poems, "Sappho in Levkas and Other Poems," was published in 1915, and his second, "In April Once," in 1920. During the World War, Mr. Percy had active service in France, having the rank of Captain.

PIPER, EDWIN FORD. Born at Auburn, Neb., Feb. 8, 1871. Spent his early youth on a farm near his native town and in various parts of the cattle country of the State. Took his degree of A.B. from the University of Nebraska in 1897 and of A.M. in 1900, and later took graduate-student work at Harvard. Mr. Piper was Instructor in English at the University of Nebraska from 1899 to 1903, when he went to Harvard, and returned to the University in the same capacity for the two years following, when he entered upon the same position at the University of Iowa, where he still remains. He has published but one collection of verse, "Barbed Wire," a volume dealing with life in the West, though he appears frequently in the magazines.

RICE, CALE YOUNG. Born at Dixon, Ky., Dec. 7, 1872. Graduated from Cumberland University in 1893 and from Harvard University in 1895, where he remained to take the degree of A.M. in 1896. He is the author of many fine poetic dramas, some of which have had successful stage presentation, and of several volumes of lyric poetry. In poetic drama his best-known works are "Charles di Tocca," 1903; "David," 1904; "Yolanda of Cyprus," 1905; "A Night in Avignon," 1907; "The Immortal Lure," 1911; and "Porzia," 1913. Of late Mr. Rice has confined himself chiefly to lyric poetry, covering a wide range of subjects, since he has traveled extensively and finds inspiration for his work in the beauty of far countries and their philosophies, as well as in the more familiar life about him. His best-known lyric collections are: "Nirvana Days," 1908; "Many Gods," 1910; "Far Quests,":

1912; "At the World's Heart," 1914; "Earth and New Earth," 1916; "Trails Sunward," 1917; "Wraiths and Realities," 1918; "Songs to A. H. R.," 1918; and "Shadowy Thresholds," 1919. With the exception of the last five titles, Mr. Rice's work, both in lyric and drama, may be found in his two volumes of "Collected Plays and Poems," 1915.

ROBINSON, CORINNE ROOSEVELT. Born in New York City in 1861. Educated by private teachers, and at Miss Comstock's School in New York, supplemented by a short period of study in Dresden. Married Douglas Robinson, 1882. Mrs. Robinson, who is a sister to Col. Theodore Roosevelt, has always taken an active part in philanthropic and political affairs, and, since her brother's death, has given much of her time to speaking upon his life and work, in the interest of Americanization. Mrs. Robinson has written several volumes of verse: "The Call of Brotherhood," 1912; "One Woman to Another," 1914; and "Service and Sacrifice," 1919. All show the fine ideals and gracious spirit of their writer.

ROBINSON, EDWIN ARLINGTON. Born at Head Tide, Maine, Dec. 22, 1869. Educated at Harvard University. Mr. Robinson is a psychological poet of great subtlety; his poems are usually studies of types and he has given us a remarkable series of portraits. He is recognized as one of the finest and most distinguished poets of our time. His successive volumes are: "Children of the Night," 1897; "Captain Craig," 1902; "The Town Down the River," 1910; "The Man Against the Sky," 1916; "Merlin," 1917; and "Launcelot," 1920. The last-named volume was awarded a prize of five hundred dollars, given by The Lyric Society for the best book manuscript offered to it in 1919. In addition to his work in poetry, Mr. Robinson has written two prose plays, "Van Zorn," and "The Porcupine."

SANDBURG, CARL. Born at Galesburg, Ill., Jan. 6, 1878. Educated at Lombard College, Galesburg. Married Lillian Steichen, of Milwaukee, 1908. Mr. Sandburg served several years as secretary to the Mayor of Milwaukee, then went to Chicago where he became associate editor of *System*, leaving this magazine to become an editorial writer upon the *Chicago Daily News*. He first came into prominence by a poem on "Chicago" published in *Poetry*, of that city, and was awarded the Levinson Prize for this poem, in 1914. The following year he published a collection of his verse under the title of "Chicago Poems," and in 1918 appeared his second volume, "Corn Huskers." This was one of two volumes to receive the Columbia University award of $500 for the best book of verse of the year. Mr. Sandburg belongs to the newer movement in poetry, using the *vers-libre* forms. He is a writer of rugged power, interested in the social aspects of modern life, but a poet who is also sensitive to beauty and a frequent master of the magic phrase.

SCHAUFFLER, ROBERT HAVEN. Born at Brün, Austria, though of American parentage, on April 8, 1879. He studied at Northwestern University, but took his degree of A.B. from Princeton, in 1902, and afterwards spent a year in study at the University of Berlin. Mr. Schauffler was a musician before he took up literature and was a pupil of several famous masters of the 'cello. He has written upon musical subjects, notably in his volume, "The Musical Amateur," and in his delightful account of his musical experiences in the Army, "Fiddler's Luck," 1920. He is also the author of several books of travel, such as "Romantic Germany," and "Romantic America," but it was with his poem, "Scum o' the Earth," published in one of the magazines in 1912, that he first came into prominence as a poet. As its name implies, it is a poem taking up the question of America's debt to the immigrant, and looking at it with the vision of the poet. This poem furnished the title to Mr. Schauffler's collection of verse, published in 1912.

SEEGER, ALAN. Born in New York City, June 22, 1888. He spent his childhood upon Staten Island, where he was constantly in sight of the great steamships of all nations moving in and out of New York Harbor — the gateway to the Western Hemisphere. Returning to Manhattan, he was sent to the Horace Mann School, but while still a lad, the family removed to Mexico where the most impressionable years of his boyhood were spent. The influence of the romantic Southern life is shown in his earliest poetry. Upon his return to America, several years later, he was prepared for college at the Hackley School at Tarrytown, N.Y., and entered Harvard in 1906, where he remained to graduate in 1910. Then followed a period of indecision as to his future work, a period of two years spent in New York, seeking some adequate outlet for the gifts which he seemed unable to bring to a practical issue. Finally, his family decided to give him a period in Paris, and he had been living there, with excursions to other parts of the Old World, for nearly two years when the Great War broke out and furnished him with the incentive to high adventure which his spirit craved. He enlisted at once and was enrolled in the Foreign Legion which was soon sent to the front. For two years he played not only a gallant part as a soldier, but, as his letters and journal show, he developed personal qualities of the noblest. Indeed no dedication made by youth to the ideal of the war was more complete than his. During his period with the Legion he wrote the poems by which he will be remembered, "Champagne, 1914," "Ode to the American Volunteers Fallen for France," and his exquisite "Rendezvous," published in this collection. All are beautiful and all have the exaltation which marked the soldier's spirit in the earlier years of the war. Not only did his poems foreshadow his own death, but they showed the willingness, almost eagerness, with which he offered himself. Although America was not yet in the war, a tardiness which had been a great grief to Alan Seeger, there is a poetic coincidence in the fact that he met his death on July 4, 1916, while the Legion was carrying out an attack on the little village of Belloy-en-Santerre. After his death two volumes, containing his poems, letters, and diary, were issued, 1917, with an Introduction by William Archer.

SHANAFELT, CLARA. Miss Shanafelt has, as yet, published no collection of poetry, but has appeared in the magazines, particularly *Poetry*, of Chicago, from whose pages we took the lyric included in this volume.

SHEPARD, ODELL. Born in Sterling, Ill., July 22, 1884. Educated at Harvard University. Is now instructor in the English department of Yale University. He is the author of "A Lonely Flute," 1917.

SMITH, MAY RILEY. Born in Rochester, N.Y., May 7, 1842. Educated at Tracey Female Institute, Rochester, and at Brockport, N.Y., Collegiate Institute. Married Albert Smith, of Springfield, Ill., in 1869. Author of "The Gift of Gentians," 1882; "The Inn of Rest," 1888; "Sometime and Other Poems," 1892. While Mrs. Smith has in recent years done work much more modern in character and finer as poetry, she is most widely known for her poem, "Sometime," written in her earlier life.

SPEYER, LEONORA. Born in Washington, D.C., in 1872. Studied music in Brussels, Paris, and Leipzig, and played the violin professionally under Nikisch, Seidl, and others. Married Sir Edgar Speyer, of London, and lived in that city until 1915, when they came to America and took up their residence in New York. Lady Speyer, who had never written poetry until her return to her native country, has since that time made for herself a place among the newer group and is doing excellent work both in the free forms and lyric.

STERLING, GEORGE. Born at Sag Harbor, N.Y., Dec. 1, 1869. Educated at private schools and at St. Charles College, Ellicott City, Md. Mr. Sterling is a poet to whom the sublimer aspects of nature and thought appeal and he has a style admirably suited to their portrayal. He is the author of "The Testimony of the Suns," 1903; "A Wine of Wizardry," 1908; "The House of Orchids," 1911; "Beyond the Breakers,"

1914; "Exposition Ode," 1915; and "Lilith, A Dramatic Poem," 1919.

STORK, CHARLES WHARTON. Born in Philadelphia, Pa., Feb. 12, 1881. Took the degree of A.B. at Haverford College, 1902; of A.M. at Harvard, 1903, and of Ph.D. at the University of Pennsylvania, 1905. He then went abroad to do research work in the universities of England and Germany, where he spent several years. In 1908 he married Elisabeth, daughter of Franz von Pausinger, artist, of Salzburg, Austria, and, returning to America, took up his work at the University of Pennsylvania, where he remained as instructor and associate professor until 1916, when he resigned to engage in literary work. Mr. Stork's first book of verse to become known was "Sea and Bay," 1916. Since then he has done a great deal of translating from the Swedish and German, having made admirable renderings of Gustaf Fröding, 1916, as well as many other Swedish poets, whose work he published in an "Anthology of Swedish Lyrics," 1917. He has since made a translation of "Selected Poems of Verner Von Heidenstam," the Nobel Prize winner of 1916. In addition to his work in Swedish poetry, he has made an excellent rendering of the lyrics of Hofmansthal, the Austrian poet. Mr. Stork is the editor and owner of *Contemporary Verse*, devoted to the poetry of the present group in America. A second collection of his own verse will soon appear.

TEASDALE, SARA. Born in St. Louis, Mo., Aug. 10, 1884. Educated at private schools. Married Ernst B. Filsinger, 1915. She is the author of "Sonnets to Duse," 1907; "Helen of Troy and Other Poems," 1911; "Rivers to the Sea," 1915; "Love Songs," 1917, which was awarded the Columbia University Prize of $500 for the best book of poems of the current year. Miss Teasdale is also the editor of "The Answering Voice; A Hundred Love Lyrics by Women," 1917. She has herself written some of the finest love songs of our period and is one of the purest and most spontaneous lyric poets of her generation.

TIETJENS, EUNICE, born Chicago, Ill., July 29, 1884. Educated in Europe, chiefly at Geneva, Dresden, and Paris. Married Paul Tietjens, musician, in 1904. Was divorced in 1914, and in 1920 married Cloyd Head, of Chicago. Was for several years associate editor of *Poetry*. Mrs. Tietjens has traveled extensively, especially in the interior of China. She also spent sixteen months in France as a war correspondent for the Chicago Daily News. Mrs. Tietjens is the author of "Profiles from China," 1917, and "Body and Raiment," 1919.

TORRENCE, RIDGELY. Born at Xenia, Ohio, Nov. 27, 1875. Educated at Miami University, Ohio, and at Princeton.

Served as assistant librarian at the Astor and Lenox Libraries in New York City from 1897 to 1903. His volumes of poetry and poetic drama include: "The House of a Hundred Lights," 1900; "El Dorado, A Tragedy," 1903; "Abelard and Héloise: A Drama," 1907. Since Mr. Torrence published his last collection, he has done some of his finest work in lyric and narrative poetry, work that has appeared in the magazines and which will probably be collected soon into book form. He is a poet of vision, one of the truest voices of our day, though his work is sparse in output.

TOWNE, CHARLES HANSON. Born at Louisville, Ky., Feb. 2, 1877. Educated at New York City College. Mr. Towne has been an active journalist, having been connected with several metropolitan magazines and successively editor of *The Smart Set, The Delineator, The Designer,* and *McClure's Magazine.* Despite his journalistic work he has found time to write several volumes of poetry largely reflective of the life of to-day and particularly of Manhattan. The best-known are: "The Quiet Singer, and Other Poems," 1908; "Manhattan," 1909; "Youth, and Other Poems," 1910; "Beyond the Stars, and Other Poems," 1912; "To-Day and To-Morrow," 1916; and "A World of Windows," 1919.

UNTERMEYER, JEAN STARR. Born at Zanesville, Ohio, in 1886. Educated in private schools of New York City and in special courses at Columbia University. Married Louis Untermeyer, the poet, 1907. Mrs. Untermeyer did not begin writing until the free verse movement was at its height, but she has done some excellent work and made a place for herself in the movement. Her volume of verse, "Growing Pains," was published in 1918.

UNTERMEYER, LOUIS. Born in New York City, Oct. 1, 1885. Educated in the public schools of that city. Mr. Untermeyer, in addition to writing poetry, has done much work in book reviewing, particularly for the *Chicago Evening Post,* and is the author of a critical book, "The New Era in American Poetry," 1919, which discusses in a stimulating manner the work of a group of poets of the day. His own volumes of poems are: "First Love," 1911; "Challenge," 1914; "And Other Poets: A Book of Parodies," 1916; "These Times," 1917; "Including Horace," another volume of parodies, 1919. Mr. Untermeyer has made an excellent translation of the "Poems of Heinrich Heine," 1917, and has edited a school anthology of "Modern American Poetry," 1919.

WALSH, THOMAS. Born in Brooklyn, Oct. 14, 1875. Educated at Georgetown University, where he took the degree of Ph.D. in 1892. Spent the years from 1892 to 1895, at Columbia University. In 1917 he received the honorary degree of

Litt. D. from Georgetown University and of LL.D. from the University of Notre Dame. He is the author of "The Prison Ships," 1909; "The Pilgrim Kings," 1915; "Gardens Overseas," 1917; and is the translator of a collection of the poems of the Nicaraguan poet, Rubén Dario. Mr. Walsh is much interested in Spanish literature and art and much of his work turns upon these themes.

WATTLES, WILLARD. Born in Bayneville, Kan., June 8, 1888. Educated at the University of Kansas, where he took the degree of A.B. in 1909 (Phi Beta Kappa) and of A.M. in 1911. Mr. Wattles took up the profession of teaching and was instructor in English at the High School, Leavenworth, Kan., 1910–11, leaving this position to go East and become one of the staff of the Massachusetts Agricultural College, where he remained until 1914, when he returned to his *alma mater*, the University of. Kansas. He is still assistant in the English department of that college. He has published as yet but one collection, "Lanterns in Gethsemane," 1917, a volume of poems pertaining to the life of Christ, but not written in the usual vein of religious poetry. He is also the compiler of "Sunflowers," a book of Kansas poems, 1916.

WHEELOCK, JOHN HALL. Born at Far Rockaway, N.Y., in 1886. He took the degree of A.B. from Harvard University in 1908 and spent the next two years in Germany, studying during 1909 at Göttingen and during 1910 at the University of Berlin. Since his return to America he has been connected with the publishing house of Charles Scribner's Sons. His first volume, "The Human Fantasy," 1911, attracted attention by the faithfulness with which it depicted the motley life of New York. His second was "The Beloved Adventure," 1912; followed by "Love and Liberation," 1913, and "Dust and Light," 1919. The last volume, from which the selections in this anthology are taken, contains some of Mr. Wheelock's finest lyrical work, work full of the passion for beauty.

WIDDEMER, MARGARET. Born at Doylestown, Pa. Educated by private teachers and at the Drexel Institute Library School of Philadelphia, where she graduated in 1909. Attention was first drawn to her work by a child-labor poem, "The Factories," which was widely quoted, the social movement in poetry being then at its height. Miss Widdemer is both poet and novelist, having published several books in each field. In poetry her work includes: "The Factories with Other Lyrics," 1915; and "The Old Road to Paradise," 1918. This volume shared with that of Carl Sandburg the Columbia University Prize of $500 for the best book of poems published in 1918. In the same year Miss Widdemer was married to

Robert Haven Schauffler, author of "Scum o' the Earth."
She is a poet of much delicacy, and several of her poems, notably "The Dark Cavalier" in this volume, are among the
best lyric work of the period.

WILKINSON, FLORENCE (MRS. WILFRID MUIR EVANS).
Born at Tarrytown, N.Y. Miss Wilkinson studied at Chicago
University and other American colleges and afterwards at
the Sorbonne and the Bibliothèque Nationale of Paris. She
is the author of several novels, of which the best known are:
"The Lady of the Flag Flowers," "The Strength of the
Hills," and "The Silent Door"; and also of one or two volumes
of plays, but her best work is found in her poetry of which
she has written two volumes: "The Far Country," 1906, and
"The Ride Home," 1913.

WILKINSON, MARGUERITE OGDEN BIGELOW. Born at
Halifax, Nova Scotia, Nov. 15, 1883. Educated at Northwestern University. Married James Wilkinson, 1909. Author
of "In Vivid Gardens," 1911; "By a Western Wayside,"
1912; "New Voices," a critical study of present-day poetry,
with a supplementary anthology, 1919; and "Bluestone," a
collection of her own poems, 1920. The title poem of this volume was awarded a prize of $150 by the Poetry Society of
America for the best poem read at its meetings during 1919.
Mrs. Wilkinson has done a great deal of journalistic work,
having conducted literary departments on various journals.

WOOD, CLEMENT. Born at Tuscaloosa, Ala., Sept. 1, 1888,
but reared in Birmingham, Ala., where he attended Taylor's
Academy and Birmingham High School. Received his degree
of A.B. from the University of Alabama in 1909, and of LL.B
from Yale University in 1911. He returned to his home city
of Birmingham and practiced law for several years, becoming
assistant city attorney of Birmingham in 1912, and police
magistrate of the Central District of Birmingham, 1912–13.
The following year he came to New York for advanced work
in sociology and literature and became a contributor of poems,
essays, and short stories to various magazines. In 1917 he
was awarded the first prize of $250 by the Newark Commit-
tee of One Hundred, as part of their Anniversary Celebration,
for his poem, "The Smithy of God," and in 1919 he was also
awarded one of the three Lyric Society Prizes, of $500 each,
for his poem, "Jehovah." In 1914 Mr. Wood married Mildred
M. Cummer, of Buffalo, N.Y., who is also a writer. In poetry
he is the author of the following books: "Glad of Earth,"
1917; "The Earth Turns South," 1919; and "Jehovah," 1920.
He has also written a novel called "Mountain," published
in 1920.

INDEX OF AUTHORS

AIKEN, CONRAD 50, 87, 99
AKINS, ZOË 52
ANDERSON, MARGARET STEELE 29, 76
ARENSBERG, WALTER CONRAD 86, 180

BAKER, KARLE WILSON 82, 90
BATES, KATHARINE LEE 13
BENÉT, STEPHEN VINCENT 164
BENÉT, WILLIAM ROSE 30, 111
BRADLEY, WILLIAM ASPINWALL 182
BRANCH, ANNA HEMPSTEAD 20, 112, 135
BURNET, DANA 120
BURR, AMELIA JOSEPHINE 54, 68
BURT, MAXWELL STRUTHERS 93
BYNNER, WITTER 62, 100, 170, 172, 209

CARLIN, FRANCIS 78, 210
CLEGHORN, SARAH N. 139
CONKLING, GRACE HAZARD 86, 167, 177
CORBIN, ALICE 143
COX, ELEANOR ROGERS 32, 73
CRAPSEY, ADELAIDE 205, 206, 207
CROMWELL, GLADYS 202

DARGAN, OLIVE TILFORD 15
DAVIES, MARY CAROLYN 6, 66, 162
DAVIS, FANNIE STEARNS 128, 191
DE CASSERES, BENJAMIN 212
DRISCOLL, LOUISE 52

FICKE, ARTHUR DAVISON 74, 205
FISHER, MAHLON LEONARD 85, 203

INDEX OF AUTHORS

O'BRIEN, EDWARD J. 163, 209
O'CONOR, NORREYS JEPHSON 77, 191
O'HARA, JOHN MYERS 202, 203, 213
O SHEEL, SHAEMAS 69
OPPENHEIM, JAMES 99, 104, 194

PEABODY, JOSEPHINE PRESTON 67, 119, 121
PERCY, WILLIAM ALEXANDER 189
PIPER, EDWIN FORD 184

RICE, CALE YOUNG 19, 25, 96, 212
ROBINSON, CORINNE ROOSEVELT 81, 177
ROBINSON, EDWIN ARLINGTON 33, 109, 145

SANDBURG, CARL 48, 179, 188, 208
SCHAUFFLER, ROBERT HAVEN 159, 169
SEEGER, ALAN 164
SHANAFELT, CLARA 20
SHEPHERD, ODELL 196
SMITH, MAY RILEY 141
SPEYER, LEONORA 83, 168
STERLING, GEORGE 48, 134, 211
STORK, CHARLES WHARTON 110, 201

TEASDALE, SARA 5, 8, 45, 84
TIETJENS, EUNICE 95
TORRENCE, RIDGELY 56, 142
TOWNE, CHARLES HANSON 55, 94, 110

UNTERMEYER, JEAN STARR 186
UNTERMEYER, LOUIS 29, 90, 134

WALSH, THOMAS 80, 120
WATTLES, WILLARD 26, 144, 173
WHEELOCK, JOHN HALL 9, 195, 205, 208
WIDDEMER, MARGARET 70, 181, 194, 199
WILKINSON, FLORENCE 175
WILKINSON, MARGUERITE 79, 115
WOOD, CLEMENT 6, 171, 192

INDEX OF AUTHORS

FLETCHER, JOHN GOULD 4, 153
FOSTER, JEANNE ROBERT 181
FROST, ROBERT 3, 91, 116, 185

GARRISON, THEODOSIA 119
GILTINAN, CAROLINE 27
GRIFFITH, WILLIAM 5, 204
GUITERMAN, ARTHUR 27, 28

H. D. 101, 102
HAGEDORN, HERMANN 158, 193
HARDING, RUTH GUTHRIE 74
HOYT, HELEN 82

JOHNS, ORRICK 18, 31, 145
JONES, THOMAS S., JR. 7, 22, 51

KEMP, HARRY 13
KILMER, ALINE 127, 132, 133
KILMER, JOYCE 12, 26, 159, 165
KREYMBORG, ALFRED 12, 98

LEE, AGNES 111, 172
LEE, MUNA 182
LEDOUX, LOUIS V. 124, 128, 132
LEONARD, WILLIAM ELLERY. 65, 199
LINDSAY, VACHEL 37, 63, 71, 157
LOWELL, AMY 72, 103, 105, 140, 178

MASTERS, EDGAR LEE 148, 196
MIDDLETON, SCUDDER 69, 76
MILLAY, EDNA ST. VINCENT 84, 188, 189
MONROE, HARRIET 14, 97
MORGAN, ANGELA 75, 170
MORTON, DAVID 3, 51, 173

NEIHARDT, JOHN G. 124
NORTON, GRACE FALLOW 47

ImTheStory.com